Samlesbury

A Short History

Alistair C. Hodge

Published by Carnegie Press, 24 Ribblesdale Place, Preston
Printed by T. Snape & Co., Bolton's Court, Preston.

PREFACE

Interest in local history abounds. To discover evidence about the lives of our ancestors can be fascinating and highly rewarding. It can also be very frustrating. All too often our research turns up more questions and mysteries than solid answers, and we begin to realise just how much we do not know, and probably will never be able to find out. However, a great deal can be discovered about most places, and new techniques are continually being developed to help the local-history detective. Fascination usually outweighs the frustration, and the search continues...

The history of Samlesbury is no exception. Samlesbury is a small, mainly rural township in central Lancashire, on the south bank of the river Ribble, between Blackburn and Preston. There is not really a village of Samlesbury, but there is a fine manor house, a delightful little church, and many other attractions for the local historian.

This little book started out life as a handbook or guide to Samlesbury Hall. In part it remains just that. But a concern to search out more of the general history soon developed - for good historical reasons, I hope, and not through self-indulgence - and the book has grown by several pages. So the reader will find that the history of Samlesbury Hall and its occupants is used here to illustrate and explain, more generally, a little about the manor and township as a whole. I hope that, in turn, this improves our understanding of the Hall. Since there are several points on which I have put forward new or modified ideas (many of them, I hasten to add, made possible through the researches of other historians in other places) I felt that I had to give references in footnotes. I hope that for the general reader these do not intrude too much. Generally, spellings in quotations have not been modernised or corrected; dates, however, have been altered where necessary to accord with the modern practice of beginning the year on January 1st.

I should like to record just a few of the debts of gratitude I have run up during the research for this book. First, to the Samlesbury Hall Trustees for allowing me to look at documents, reproduce illustrations and to wander through the Hall at length; to Mr. Brown for his help and kind permission to reproduce some of Robert Eaton's illustrations which are now in his possession; to the many farmers and their families who allowed me to tramp their fields in search of old field boundaries, an elusive deer park and the ubiquitous ridge and furrow. I would like to thank the staffs of the Lancashire Record Office and the Harris Reference Library, Preston. Once again, their help was invaluable.

Copyright © Alistair Hodge, 1985
First edition, April, 1985
Second edition, February, 1986

ISBN 0 948789 04 2

PRE-HISTORY

Dim, distant and very murky - quite an appropriate way to begin describing the very early history of Samlesbury, indeed of Lancashire as a whole. The lack of surviving evidence really does bring down a blanket of fog over the work of the local historian. The mist hides an immense amount of information about the lives of our more distant ancestors. The first written reference we have to Samlesbury tells us that the manorial lord in 1190 was one Gospatric, son of Swain, perhaps himself a younger son of Leofwin from Hindley near Wigan. We are told that he had 14 bovates[a] of land - about 250-280 acres - in 1196 and that his heirs general also owned land in Elston, or Alston, across the Ribble.[1]

However, just because this is the first written reference we have to a manor of Samlesbury, it would be dangerous to assume that the area had previously been deserted. It is unlikely that Gospatric was the first resident in Samlesbury. I say this because of what we know about the Ribble Valley generally in pre-Conquest times. Archaeological evidence in particular has always been plentiful from the valley. First there are

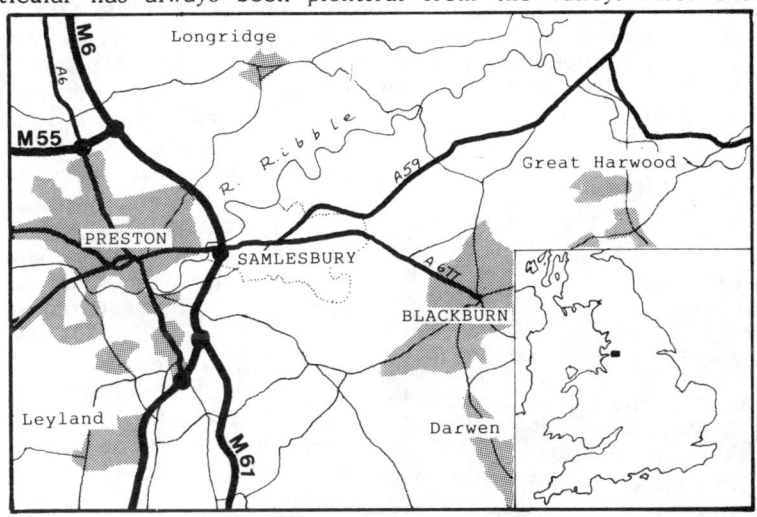

Map of part of central Lancashire showing the location of Samlesbury. The dotted line indicates the township boundary.

Ribchester (the Roman fort of Bremetennacum) and the smaller Roman station at Walton-le-Dale.[2] Not only did both these camps control major routes from south to north, but they also lay on a very important east-west route. This route, which follows the valleys of the Ribble and the Aire, crosses the Pennines at one of their lowest and easiest points. Later, we know that this route linked the two Viking centres of York and Dublin - a most important confirmation of these links comes in the form of the Cuerdale hoard, a cache of over 7,000 silver coins and other

---

[a]*bovate:* a measurement of land, usually reckoned as the amount of land that an ox could plough in a year; an oxgang of land.

N.B. *Numbered foot-note references are given at the back, from page 42.*

objects discovered in the southern bank of the Ribble in 1840, just downstream from Samlesbury, in the neighbouring township. It is thought that they had been buried there in about 900 A.D..[3]

Before Roman times, even, there is plenty of evidence for human settlement from various parts of the lower Ribble. Walton-le-Dale, Fishwick and Penwortham have all yielded evidence of early human influence; Higher Brockholes, just across the river from Samlesbury, has thrown up several finds from the Bronze Age and earlier. One recent authority feels that Preston itself might possibly have been an early British tribal centre of some kind.[4] Dig almost anywhere in the Ribble Valley, it appears, and more evidence comes to light. Traditionally, and with some justification, early Lancashire has been seen as a backwater, a land of forests, marshes and wild beasts. In some old-fashioned books, the latter almost seems to include the humans, who are described variously as 'barbaric', 'uncouth' or 'primitive'. Thankfully, more recent interpretations take a more favourable view of the first Britons and their achievements. The environment of Lancashire was certainly hostile, wet and cold, but the people were probably no more 'wild' than we are. Almost every new archaeological find adds, not only to our understanding of these past societies, but also to the respect we feel for them. As one writer has put it, 'the average Bronze Age male possessed the mental and physical attributes necessary for entry into most modern occupations, and dressed in modern garb he would not attract a second glance in the supermarket queue.'[5]

This peaceful, snow-covered track through the Samlesbury woodland is still a public footpath, but it shows little sign of its former importance - it used to be the busy main road from Samlesbury Hall to the church and the ferry.

To date, there has not been a great deal of archaeological work done in the Samlesbury area. We cannot be sure that the area was peopled in early times. We do not know if there was any early settlement here or not. However, knowing that the Preston area has been a major crossroads for at least 2,500 years, it does not seem improbable.

A useful first clue is often provided by the place name itself. The whole township is called Samlesbury (pronounced 'Samz-bury'), and the name has been spelt in many different ways over the centuries. When the name first appears on record, in the twelfth century, it is spelt 'Samelesbure'. The modern spelling was used as early as the fourteenth century. What does the name mean? If the first half of the name originally

Another view of the same track, quite near the later Catholic chapel on the hill above the main Preston - Blackburn turnpike road. It was the building of this road in the 1820s that made the track obsolete. Note how centuries of use have lowered the level of the track in comparison with the field to the right.

began in 'Sh' (and in the thirteenth century it was sometimes written as 'Schampelesbyri' or 'Schamelesbyre'), it may be derived from the Old English 'sceamol', meaning a bench or ledge. Ekwall gives this as the most likely derivation of the name, and points out that there is such a ledge around Samlesbury church, where the land is slightly higher than the surrounding river bank. Place names, however, are rarely that simple, and many other theories have been put forward, some more plausible than others. Is it not possible that it is called after a man called Samuel who lived here, hence 'Samuels-bury'? Perhaps. Or, did it not refer to the excellent fishing in the Ribble, hence 'Salmon-bury'? Well, probably not. How about the Romans? Perhaps they saw this spot and decided that it was very beautiful (belisima), hence 'Belisimas-bury'? This is probably the least likely derivation yet suggested. But one can never be sure. Perhaps the place name is not all that useful in this case after all.[6]

Detail from carved window sill on Samlesbury Hall, supposedly showing a Roman Emperor.

If Ekwall is correct, then the Old English derivation of the name may suggest that there was indeed an established settlement near the church before the Norman Conquest. Samlesbury was not mentioned in the Domesday book of 1086-7, but the survey for this part of the country is very sketchy and probably incomplete. A hundred years later Samlesbury makes, through its lord Gospatric, its first undramatic entry on the stage of recorded history; from this point the historical record is unbroken, though incomplete.[7]

THE MEDIEVAL MANOR OF SAMLESBURY

It seems likely that Gospatric and his immediate successors lived in a manor house somewhere close to the river Ribble, perhaps near the church or by the site of the later (and now ruined) Lower Hall. Samlesbury Higher Hall, the familiar half-timbered and brick building by the main Preston to Blackburn road, dates from somewhat later, although there was probably an earlier hall on the same site.

It was by the river that Samlesbury chapel, St. Leonard-the-Less, was built. Perhaps originally endowed by Gospatric in the twelfth century, this chapel was a chapel of ease to the parish church of St. Leonard, Walton-le-Dale (hence the Samlesbury chapel's name), and the original church was probably on the same site as the present Samlesbury church. Parts of the gable walls of an earlier building, apparently of the fourteenth century, can still be seen. It seems probable that Gospatric's manor house was fairly close to this church.[1]

There is no trace of the first Samlesbury Hall today. In his book on Samlesbury, Robert Eaton suggested a site about quarter of a mile downstream from the later Lower Hall where, he says, there are 'ancient stone foundations' close to the river and right next to a ford which would have led to Gospatric's other holdings in Elston.[2] I have not been able to trace the foundations which Eaton said were quite visible 50 years ago, but the site he describes is certainly a contender. Unfortunately, perhaps, the low-lying land by the river is productive farm land, and intensive farming over the years will make it ever more difficult to trace the site of the first Hall. The very quality of this land is significant - the best agricultural land was down here by the river and the first lords of the manor would surely have had first choice of the available land. One final point suggestive of a site near the river is the fact that a large number of other Ribble Valley manor houses were built there. Balderston, Osbaldeston, Old Hall at Ribchester, Salesbury and several others were each built on the southern bank of the Ribble.

Gospatric had four sons and a daughter. He was succeeded before 1212 by Roger who had married Margaret, daughter and heiress to Walter de Clifton. Roger de Samlesbury was in turn succeeded by his son, William. This William and his wife, Avina, failed to produce a male heir and on William's death the Samlesbury estates were divided between their three daughters, Margery, Cecily and Elizabeth, and their respective husbands (see table 1). This failure of the male line was crucial and it has helped to determine the patterns of landholding in the township ever since.[3]

The eldest of William de Samlesbury's daughters, Margery, married twice but had no children from either marriage; she died quite young and, after protracted lawsuits which lasted for nearly twenty years, her third of the property was divided between her two sisters and their husbands.[4] Thus Cecily, who had married John Deuyas some time before 1259, and Elizabeth, who married Robert de Holand (or Holland), each held one half (or 'moiety') of the manor. The manor was still split 400 years later.

Which family lived at Samlesbury? Who was lord of the manor, and

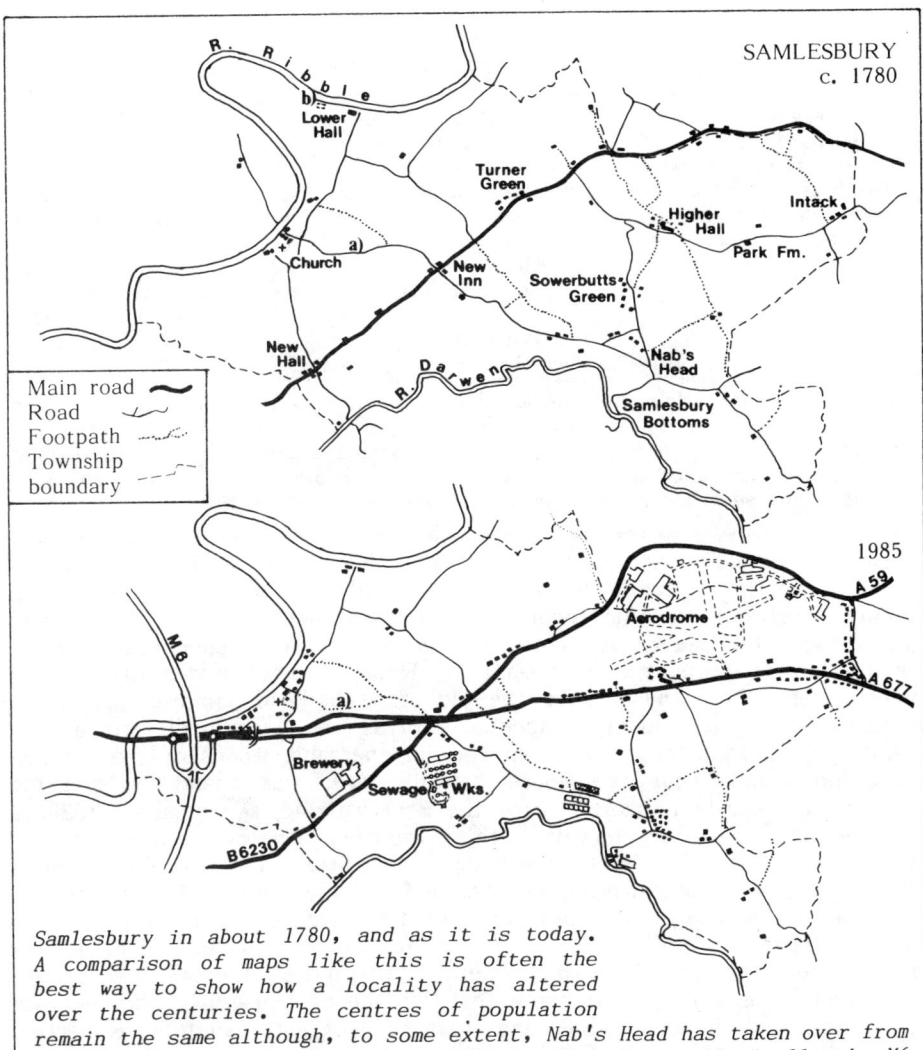

Samlesbury in about 1780, and as it is today. A comparison of maps like this is often the best way to show how a locality has altered over the centuries. The centres of population remain the same although, to some extent, Nab's Head has taken over from Sowerbutts Green. There are more main roads today - principally the M6 and the A677 Preston - Blackburn turnpike of 1824 which traverses the township and passes right by Samlesbury Hall. Note how the A59 was moved to skirt the aerodrome, but how the township boundary remains where it was. Note also the 'ribbon development' along the A677.

    a) shows the old road, pictured on pages 2 and 3.

    b) shows the rough location of Eaton's 'old stone foundations', which he takes to be the remains of the very first Samlesbury Hall.

    N.B. Representation of a footpath does not imply right of way.

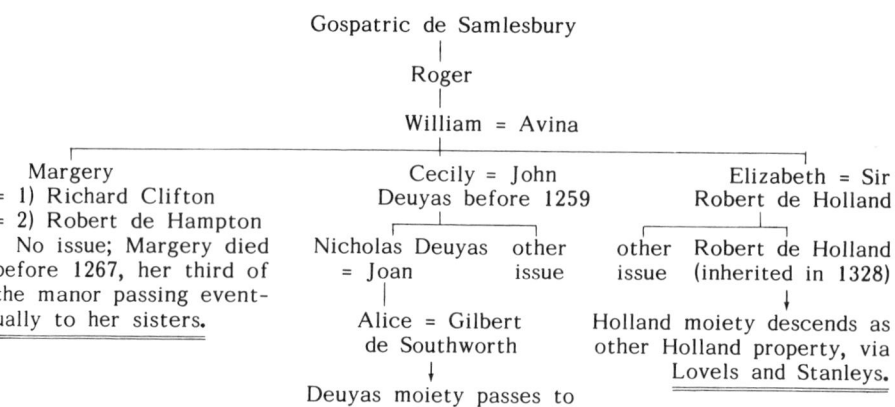

Table 1. A much simplified genealogical table, showing how the manor of Samlesbury descended. The crucial period was the second half of the 13th century, when the manor was divided. Only the Deuyas family and, later, the Southworths lived here permanently, but for a time at least there were probably two separate manor houses, one on each half of the manor.

occupied the old manor house? The usual theory has it that only one of the two families actually lived on their Samlesbury estates - the Deuyas family. According to this theory, the Hollands never lived in Samlesbury and it was the Deuyas family who occupied the old manor house by the river. Until, that is, the Scottish king, Robert Bruce, raided the area at midsummer, 1322, and 'burned the old stone hall' in Samlesbury. This is supposed to have induced Nicholas Deuyas to move house to a new building in a secluded clearing in the impenetrable woods of the Samlesbury hinterland. Thus the house by the river was abandoned and the Higher Hall was built shortly after the Scottish raid, say in about 1325.[5]

As we shall see, however, this traditional theory does not fit all the known facts. The issue hinges on the position of the Holland family. The family originated in Upholland, and quickly rose to prominence in the county's affairs in the thirteenth century. During the reign of Edward II, Sir Robert de Holland was the Earl of Lancaster's right-hand man in Lancashire. Through that employment, he acquired manors and estates throughout the county. We know that his manor house in Upholland was being fortified in about 1308, and it is not suggested that Sir Robert or his father (Elizabeth de Samlesbury's husband) ever took up permanent residence in Samlesbury.[6] Samlesbury was just one of an increasing number of manors owned by the family. However, they certainly took an active interest in their estates in Samlesbury; one collection of early transcripts contains many documents indicating the extent of their involvement in the manor's affairs. The Hollands were certainly not negligent absentee landlords.[7]

Sir Robert de Holland's connections with, and dependence upon, the Earl of Lancaster were too great for him to avoid the effects of the failure of the Earl's rebellion against Edward II. Although Holland held

Left: A gable wall of the church of St. Leonard-the-Less, Samlesbury. The line of the older, 14th-century wall can still be seen clearly, in stone of a different colour.
Below: The old font from the churchyard. It could well be older than the date on it implies.

back from the final step of fighting at the Earl's side at Boroughbridge, his estates were confiscated for his part in the rebellion, forfeit to the crown.[8] Thus we find Holland's Samlesbury estates being administered in 1322 by two royal officials, John Travers and Robert de Notyngham.[9] From exactly this period there survive two documents which tell a great deal about Sir Robert de Holland's connections with Samlesbury.

Both of these documents date from the period immediately after the seizure of Sir Robert de Holland's lands. In 1321, one of the deputy sheriffs, Robert de Leybourn, removed certain moveable goods from several of Holland's properties, including Samlesbury, under pretence of a royal warrant.[10] The local inhabitants took Leybourn to court, and he was accused of having taken

> 'and removed from the king's goods which had belonged to Robert de Holond at Samesbury 56 lances worth 14s., 26 pole-axes worth 6s. 6d., 6 shields and 3 basinets[a] worth 13s. 6d., 6 old leather sacks, 9 belts with buckles worth 6½d., 2 white horse hides worth 12d., 4 old bridles, one old rope worth 2d., 3 pairs of ploughs with irons worth 18d., 2 harrows with iron fittings worth 20d., one linen cloth worth 6d., 2 waggons worth 12d., 2 quarters of wheat worth 2 marks[b], 2 quarters 5 bushels of barley worth 12s 6d., and 35 quarters of oats worth 106s. 6d.'[11]

This list of items taken from Holland's property in Samlesbury mentions military equipment, including lances and pole-axes; it also lists agricultural produce - wheat, barley and oats - and agricultural equipment, including ploughs and harrows. That Holland had such items in Samlesbury

---
[a]*basinet*: a small, light steel head-piece, closed in front with a visor.
[b]*mark*: equivalent to 13s. 4d., or $\frac{2}{3}$ of the £ sterling. Originally a measure of the weight of silver; now obsolete except historically.

7

is very significant, and it probably indicates that he had some kind of house or farm there.

A similar conclusion comes from the list of goods stolen from the same part of Samlesbury by Scottish raiders under Robert Bruce, only a few months later, at midsummer 1322. An inquest at Penwortham on 20 January, 1324, was told that

'goods and chattels of the king in the manor of Samlesbury, which was Robert de Holande's, and by his forfeiture came to the king's hand, were taken by the Scots and carried away towards Scotland, and wholly dispersed by the sudden coming of the said Scots and not by the negligence of William de Holdene then keeper of the manor, viz:

2 wains	4 shillings
18 oxen	13s. 4d. each
55 aketones[c]	£11 0s. 0d.
100 lances	20s. 0d.
30 polhaches[d]	10s. 0d.
4 poor saddles for rounceys[e]	4s. 0d.
4 reins for rounceys	12d.
4 poor targes ['targia'][f]	4d.
2 vestments for the chapel	12s. 0d.
a chalice	10s. 0d.
a missal	6s. 8d.
a psalter	2s. 0d.
7 brassen pots, large & small	53s. 4d.
a bowl	18d.
a laver	12d.
a pan	12d.
a coverlet for a bed	2s. 0d.
3 cloths for covering beds	3s. 0d.
2 sheets	20s. 0d.'[12]

This list confirms that the Holland family owned agricultural equipment, including a large number of oxen (then almost universally used for ploughing), and a large store of military hardware, with lances for 100 men. The mention of domestic apparel - sheets, coverlets and various pots - also indicates that there was probably a manorial farm or house on Holland's lands in Samlesbury. William de Holden is named as keeper of the manor ('tunc custodis manerii'). He and his wife Alice were certainly present in Samlesbury during the Scottish raid - William may, in fact, have been killed - and they may well have lived in the Hollands' house there, looking after Sir Robert's moiety of the manor.[13]

So, if the Hollands had a manor house, or at least a large farmstead complete with arsenal, in Samlesbury, where does this leave the owner of the other moiety of the manor? It seems beyond doubt that Nicholas

---

[c]*aketone*: a knightly undergarment. Usually written 'acton', this was a padded jerkin worn under the mail; later, a leather jacket, plated with mail.
[d]*polhache*: presumably a pole-axe of some kind.
[e]*rouncy or rouncey*: from medieval Latin *'roncinus'*, a horse, especially a riding horse.
[f]*targe*: a shield, specifically, a slight shield or buckler, used especially by footmen or archers.

Deuyas did live on his Samlesbury lands. If so, could there have been two manor houses in Samlesbury, one for each half of the manor?

The territorial division of the manor was probably never very tidy. Both families could well have held lands all over the township, and the situation will have been further confused by the subsequent splitting of the third portion in about 1296. However, there is some evidence to suggest that Holland's lands were concentrated in the west of the township, near the river, and that the Deuyas estates lay mainly on the higher ground to the east of the township.

As we have seen, it was Holland's lands that Bruce attacked - the raiders came from the Preston direction and the lower part of Samlesbury near the river was the most accessible. The raiders took items from the chapel, also located by the river. We also know about a series of disagreements late in the thirteenth century between Sir Robert de Holland and the Abbots of Stanlaw (the monks who later built Whalley Abbey) concerning access to the monastery's tithe barn ('grangia') at Longlegh in Samlesbury. In 1292, Holland promised to allow the monks free access with carts and waggons through his land; this tithe barn was located quite near the church, again suggesting that Holland's lands lay in that area.[14] That the Deuyas' estates lay towards the eastern part of the township is suggested by several pieces of evidence, not least the fact that they owned Samlesbury Higher Hall, which is situated in that part of the township. The family also held lands in Mellor, adjacent to the eastern part of Samlesbury.[15] More generally, we know that the manor was still split along these lines as late as the eighteenth century; the two parts were sometimes referred to as the 'Over' and the 'Lower Hall' demesnes. Although the courts leet were held jointly, the division was still recognised.[16]

Following Holland's forfeiture in 1322, his lands in Samlesbury were leased to Nicholas Deuyas for three years - further indication that previously the two holdings had been separate - but after Holland was illegally executed in 1328 his forfeiture was reversed and his son, Robert de Holland, inherited his father's estates, including Samlesbury.[17] This half of Samlesbury descended in the same way as the other Holland lands. At about the same time, Nicholas Deuyas settled his own half of the

One of the first pictures we have of Samlesbury Higher Hall, dating from some time before 1830. It shows the main south wing to the left, with the Great Hall and its projecting bay window to the right. Most of this hall was built in the 15th and 16th centuries although there may well have been an earlier hall on the site. Picture by courtesy of Mr L Brown.

manor on his daughter Alice and her husband Gilbert de Southworth.[18] Thus the Southworths came to hold that part of Samlesbury which included the Higher Hall until they were forced by poverty to sell out in 1679. For a time they also held the Lower Hall demesne, but sold this in the early seventeenth century, apparently because of financial difficulties.[19]

The Southworth family came from the township in south Lancashire from which they took their name. They did not sell their hall at Southworth until the seventeenth century, but they lived at Samlesbury throughout. One reason for this may have been the prosperity of their new lands. Most of the land in the township today is turned over to permanent pasture, but there is evidence that arable farming was much more important here in the later medieval period than it is today. Sir Robert de Holland had no fewer than 18 oxen, as well as a large store of wheat, barley and oats, in Samlesbury. The best land may be on the low-lying river plain, but even the more sticky slopes of the higher ground are relatively good. A recent survey comments on these 'Salop series' soils: 'Given proper drainage the soils are very productive of a wide range of crops, although their rather fine texture and slow natural drainage favour grassland farming'.[20] H. B. Rodgers has found evidence that the Ribble Valley was an important part of the central arable belt of Lancashire, a conclusion similar to that of R. Cunliffe Shaw for a slightly earlier period.[21] On the ground, too, many fields in Samlesbury show the obvious signs of past arable farming. On the slopes of almost every part of the township, ridge and furrow marks can be seen. These invariably run up the slopes, and were probably created quite deliberately, as a by-product of ploughing, in order to improve the drainage, and thus the yield, of the land. The fact that most of these ridge and furrow marks are quite straight and narrow suggests they are fairly recent. Nevertheless, it shows that these lands certainly can support arable farming.[22] Some of these fields were cultivated during the last war.

In the Exchequer Lay Subsidy tax of 1332, Samlesbury was taxed at the third highest rate in Blackburn hundred, and had the second highest number of people (after Walton-le-Dale) liable to pay the tax. This is a useful indicator of the township's relative wealth, and it is confirmed by several other sources.[23]

One of the slopes to the west of Samlesbury, clearly displaying ridge and furrow marks.

Part of the township's prosperity may well have come from supplying produce for the market at Preston. The Southworths were usually prominent out-burgesses of the borough, ranked immediately after the Hoghtons; Preston was one of the earliest and most important of Lancashire's markets, and Samlesbury's proximity to it must have been significant.[24] There was a ferry across the Ribble which operated from just upstream of Samlesbury church. An eighteenth-century boathouse still exists, although the ferry was discontinued in about 1824 when the Higher Brockholes bridge was built as part of the new Preston to Blackburn turnpike road.[25]

Another Samlesbury field. At some time in the past, clearly, this was farmed as arable land.

If medieval Samlesbury was prosperous, then most of its lords were also wealthy and prominent. We have noticed Sir Robert de Holland's importance in the county's politics under Edward II. At much the same time, Sir John Deuyas was M.P. for Lancashire from 1295-8, and his son, Nicholas, was summoned to attend the Great Council at Westminster. The Southworths were hardly less distinguished. At the time that he married Alice Deuyas, Gilbert de Southworth was high sheriff of Lancashire, an office he served from July 1323 until March 1326. Around this time, too, he was sub-commissioner for the Lay Subsidy; his son, also called Gilbert, served for two years as Keeper of the Royal Forest. As prominent knights, several members of the Southworth family undertook military service; perhaps the most prominent was John Southworth, 'chivaler', who served in France during the Agincourt campaign, and succumbed to dyssentry at the siege of Harfleur in 1415. Later, other members of the family were to distinguish themselves in service against the French and the Scots.[26]

The Ribble at Samlesbury. What remains of the Lower Hall lies hidden behind the trees on the left bank, slightly closer to the river than the later farm buildings which can be seen. The 'old stone foundations' described by Eaton as being quite visible in 1936 lie somewhere further along, on the same bank, near the Alston ford which was just off the right-hand edge of this photograph. The aqueduct in the foreground confused me rather, until an early O.S. map showed that it carried Manchester Corporation's Thirlmere water main.

SIR THOMAS SOUTHWORTH AND SAMLESBURY HALL

Apart from the occasional public and military service, the Southworths probably led a fairly quiet life at Samlesbury, although few details have come down to us. From the sixteenth century, more documents survive. From this time, too, we can tell what Samlesbury Hall looked like. For these reasons, I would like to pause here to describe the hall and its surroundings.

Of the very first hall on the Higher Hall site there would appear to be no trace whatever. The oldest part of the present complex is the Great Hall - that large, open-roofed room on the western side of the old courtyard (now the main front lawn); this is the room with the bay window at its southern end. This oldest part probably replaced an earlier building. As we have seen, the Deuyas family was probably settled on this half of Samlesbury from the middle of the thirteenth century, when the manor was first divided, and the first building on this site might well have dated from then. The present Great Hall was built later, in the fifteenth century, and has been modified at several times.[1] The west wall of the Great Hall was replaced in stone with a new fireplace and chimney, probably in the sixteenth century. Perhaps at the same time, the bay window together with its small room above was added.

Sir Thomas Southworth inherited the family lands in Samlesbury in 1517 when his father John died. He served in Scotland where he was knighted in 1523, but he is better remembered as the man who rebuilt large parts of Samlesbury Hall. The Great Hall was modified and the whole south wing (or 'range') was rebuilt. When Sir Thomas died in 1546, the main parts of Samlesbury Hall which can be seen today were in existence. Substantial restorations were required, however, in the 1830s and again in the 1860s to reverse the hall's decay after a century and a half of neglect - so much so that little of the detail which can be seen today is entirely original. However, as the Preservation Committee wrote in 1925, 'It is true that the building has been extensively restored, but even this restoration has had time to take on a venerable and harmonious appearance'.

Sir Thomas Southworth had the south range built in timber, but the southern side (nearest the road) was faced in brick. Pevsner says that this is the first recorded use of brick for a manor house in Lancashire. Most of this wall as seen today is original, although the western end was extended in 1862. The brick facing was apparently added either at the same time as the range itself was built, or only slightly later. The brick facing really just encases the timber framing - which was left exposed on the other side of the building facing the original courtyard. The brick wall might well have been needed to support the weight of the bulky square-headed windows on that side. One of these, at the eastern extremity, lights a room that used to be the domestic chapel; it is said that this one came from the ruins of Whalley Abbey which, of course, was closed down by Henry VIII at just this time. This is quite possible - perhaps, in fact, Sir Thomas had seen (and measured?) the window while visiting the abbey in his official capacity, as a royal commissioner surveying the wealth of the Lancashire monasteries before they were to

The contrast between these two pictures, from 1814 and 1985 respectively, is striking. The poor state of repair that the Hall was in at the beginning of the 19th century is very evident. No wonder that so much had to be repaired and restored to save the Hall from ruin. It can be seen just how much of the fabric is new. The 1814 picture can tell us a great deal. Note how the Great Hall (on the right) has been shortened, and how it used to have at least one door, but no windows on this side. The south range (left) was extended at this end in 1865, when the new chimnies were added. [1814 picture by courtesy of Mr L. Brown.]

be closed down.[2] Also, brick was just becoming fashionable for building chimnies, and there are three (four since 1862) splendid chimnies, all on that side of the building.

The exact layout of the interior of the hall at this time is unknown. Generally, the locations of the rooms today seem to follow their original pattern. The inside of the Great Hall has been altered at both ends, but it has always been the single open room that we see today. The south range has always consisted of two storeys except at its eastern end where the chapel (later a library) extended up through both floors; the chapel was overlooked by a first-floor gallery, perhaps used by the lord and his family while watching divine service. This chapel was probably on the same site as the earlier one licenced by the authorities in 1420. Beyond this, we cannot be sure. There exists a useful description of what the hall looked like just before the first bout of nineteenth-century restoration, but even by this time there had been no resident lord for 150 years, during which time the hall was occupied by several tenants who, quite naturally, altered the internal arrangements to suit their own needs.[3]

13

Wooden relief sculpture on a window lintel, supposedly of Sir Thomas Southworth, c 1545.

We are very fortunate, however, in having a domestic inventory of the hall and its outbuildings, appended to the will of Thomas Southworth esquire and dated 1623. It lists the contents of the various rooms in some detail. Though it does not describe the building itself, it is an extremely useful document.[4]

The inventory begins with a detailed and impressive list of agricultural equipment and livestock - reminding us, of course, that a manor house of this period was not simply a family mansion, but the focal point of a relatively large-scale farming operation. Thus, there were ploughs, carts, '3 harrows with teeth & 3 without', and tools and tackle of all sorts. It is interesting that the very first item on the inventory is the family's two oxen; unfortunately the document is damaged at this point, so that we cannot tell how much these valuable animals were worth. After the oxen came '5 kyne[a] & one heiffer', '3 calves', 'four heiffers & one bull', and a total of 12 horses, some pigs and some sheep. This list would probably only include the animals found by the surveyors at the hall itself. The farm buildings included two stables, one of which - 'the litle stable' - had some kind of living accommodation above it, presumably for a fairly important servant or guest since it contained a feather bed and other furniture to the value of 44 shillings. There were also two barns, an 'oxenhouse', 'workhouses' and a brewhouse. It has usually been thought that most of these outbuildings were incorporated within the main hall complex, perhaps in the form of a north wing corresponding to the south one which still exists. This may well be the case. Samlesbury Hall was moated, and it would be logical to include most of the important buildings within its compass. There are no traces of any north range, however, and we may have to ask the archaeologists

The splendid fireplace in the Great Hall of Samlesbury Hall. This fireplace was covered up for a time, and has only been re-exposed quite recently. It probably dates from the 16th century, perhaps being built by Sir Thomas Southworth in the 1530s when he did so much other work to the Great Hall.

14   [a]*kyne*: a dialect word for cattle.

to confirm its existence.[5]

The inventory then moves on to catalogue the goods found in the main buildings. The range of items is striking. Also noticeable is the large number of beds. 32 beds are listed in all. They range from the feather beds complete with luxurious coverings and embroidered valances to 'a truckle bed' in the 'inner chamber'. In 1592 a list of 36 people living at Samlesbury Hall was drawn up.[6] This list included several members of the Southworth family, one Walter Sidweeke, their butler, John Singleton, keeper of the park, John Snape, cook, and Lawrence Bownon, porter. Of the rest, 2 were described as 'servingman', 22 were 'labourers' and 3 were described as 'spinster'. There was quite a significant little community at Samlesbury Hall.

Our 1623 inventory tells us a little more about the sleeping arrangements. Apparently, many of the servants and farm workers slept more or less where they worked. We have noted the room above 'the litle stable'. 'In the deyhouse [b] chamber' there was 'one paire of bedstocks & a litle trest[le]', while there was a bed in the 'milne' which, judging by its contents, may actually have been a smithy. Three more beds were in a 'servants chamber'. In total there were 9 feather beds and a large amount of linen and bed 'coverings', some of it quite valuable. The linen included 13 table cloths, 8 'towells' and 74 table napkins of various descriptions. There are several references to curtains and carpets, usually in family apartments like 'my lords chamber', 'Mrs. [mistress's] closett', 'the nursery' and 'the litle chamber within the nursery'.

Several rooms are mentioned by name. Unfortunately, it is rarely possible to work out exactly where they were. Inventories such as this are usually methodical, and the survey sometimes progresses around the house from room to room in a way that we can still follow today.[7] In the Samlesbury document, the farm buildings are mentioned first, followed by a lengthy list of the household linen.

A fairly recent relief of Henry VIII, now above one of the dining room doors in Samlesbury Hall. Under this king, the Southworths reached the height of their family's fortunes.

Then come references to 'the ould chamber'. If it is safe to assume that the goods listed after each room were found inside that room, then the old chamber was a large bedchamber with 6 beds, a large amount of bed linen and other furniture. Next comes the 'inner chamber', a smaller room with 2 beds. Perhaps we may assume that these rooms were located near the previously mentioned farm buildings, on the northern side of the Hall complex, although the list of expensive items contained in them suggests

---

[b]*deyhouse*: a dialect word for a dairy.

Right: Lintel from window displaying the sacred monogram IHS [a Greek abbreviation for JESUS], probably indicating where the chapel originally was.

Left: The Whalley Abbey window. Located at the eastern end of the south range, and lighting the domestic chapel, it is quite likely that this window was taken from Whalley Abbey when it was dissolved and demolished in the 1540s, just at the time when Sir Thomas Southworth was rebuilding the Hall.

Below: The south range from the east, showing the domestic chapel at the end; the Whalley window is on the other side of the building.

that they were probably for the use of members of the family.

The next room mentioned in the inventory is 'the entry', which could well refer to the entrance of the main Hall buildings themselves, perhaps even the same entrance hall that we use today. There follows a curious reference to 'new buildings' and an adjacent chamber, which appear only to be small storerooms or cupboards. The Great Hall, described simply as 'the hale', is treated near the end of the document, together with the service rooms - kitchen, larder etc. - which we know were located behind its southern end. With the outbuildings mentioned first, and 'the hale' mentioned last, it might be reasonable, by process of elimination, to regard the domestic rooms in between as referring to the only other part of the Hall that we know existed - the south range. These rooms included the mistress's 'closett', the nursery and its adjacent chamber, a servant's chamber, the 'chapell chamber', 'my lords chamber', the dining chamber, another bed chamber, the 'staire head chamber' and 'the deyhouse [dairy] chamber'.

We begin to encounter problems when we try to decide where each of these rooms was located. Some of them are fairly straight forward. The 'chapell chamber' would have been next to the chapel, which we know was at the eastern end of the south range. Perhaps it refers to the first-floor room which overlooked the chapel below. In it there were at least five beds and other furniture, so it must have been a fairly large room. The 'staire head chamber' was smaller, with only one bed; it could have been at the top of any of the two or three staircases in the main building; it could even have been the small room above the bay window, which is reached by way of a small flight of steps. We may presume that the 'deyhouse chamber' was somewhere near the dairy, which is mentioned immediately after it in the inventory. For the same reason, it is probably fair to assume that the nursery was next to the 'mistress's closett'. Many of the other rooms are almost impossible to locate accurately.

Above: The drive, looking away from the Hall. In the foreground, it follows the line of the moat, which then swings round to the right to encircle the Hall.

Below: The old courtyard of the Hall from the moat steps, now the main drive.

There was a 'dyninge chamber' listed among the main domestic apartments, and the inventory places it immediately after 'my lords chamber', perhaps suggesting that it was a small, private dining room for the family. One recent theory says that Samlesbury Hall, like others in Lancashire, was built on the 'unit system', whereby the whole complex was divided between two or three branches of the family, living more or less separately.[8] Apart from a few architectural details, there would appear to be little direct evidence of this in the case of Samlesbury Hall. The separate dining chamber might support this theory, although its contents are fairly sparse - 'one longe table & 2 cupboards, 2 chaires, 3 quishions[c] 3 carpetts'. In it there was no plate or pewter, all of which, apparently, was still kept in the Great Hall.

We cannot be sure if the Southworths still ate in the Great Hall, or if they had abandoned that large and draughty room for the comfort of a more private apartment. The answer could well be a compromise

---

[c]*quishion*: an early spelling of the word *cushion*.

– that they ate in the Hall on special occasions or when there were guests, and that they took their everyday meals in the private dining room. It is worth noting fully the items found in the Great Hall:

'Item, in the hale: 2 tables, one rugge and a forme[d]   26s. 4d.
Item, one settle   3s. 4d.
Item, 126 peeces of pewter beinge in weight 117 pounds at eight pence the pound   £3 18s. 0d.
Item, pott brasse; 6 peeces in weight 117 pounds   39s. 0d.
Item, 12 peeces of panne brasse & candlesticke brasse in weight 22 pounds   16s. 8d.'

This list mentions a substantial amount of pewter and brass, together with some furniture. It is usually thought that at least some of the plate would have been displayed in the bay window recess – certainly, there is no mention of a cupboard in the room. In fact, the inventory gives the impression that the room was quite sparsely furnished.

In part, this may be because the inventory omits some of the semi-permanent furniture and fittings. We know that there was a splendid and fantastic passage screen which used to be placed at the northern end of the Great Hall. This moveable screen, which is dated 1532, was similar in appearance to that of Rufford; it was dismantled early in the nineteenth century. Parts of it were included with other old pieces of woodwork to create the 'minstrels' gallery' above the southern end of the hall. Several inscriptions from the old passage screen can still be read there. It was at this southern end of the hall that the main table would have been located, elevated on a dais which was still to be seen as late as 1830.[9] The Great Hall has been altered in other ways too. At the northern end the hall has been shortened by about a half of one bay and there have been other slight modifications at the other end, under the minstrels' gallery. The effect of these changes has been to shorten

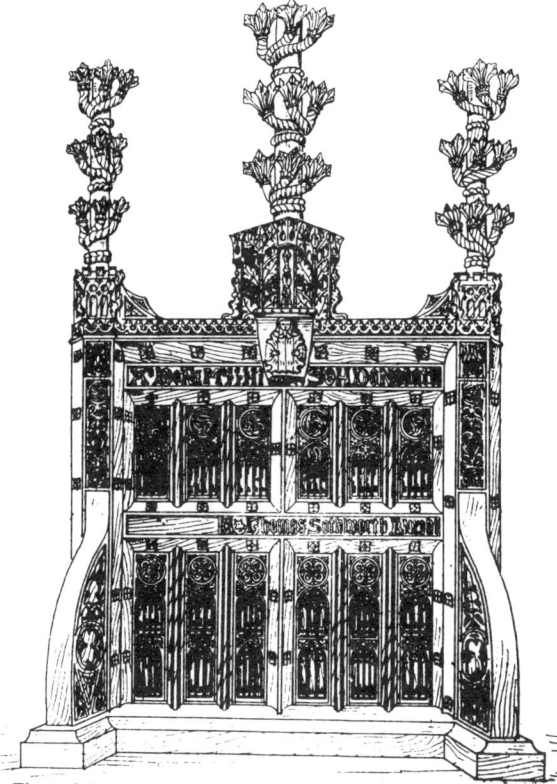

The old passage screen that used to stand in the Great Hall. From a sketch by Rev. S.J. Allen, made about the year 1833.

---

[d]*forme*: a long seat without a back.

the whole of the Great Hall by about 10 or 12 feet.

The 1623 inventory gives us a fascinating glimpse of Samlesbury Hall not long after the present buildings were completed. The picture it gives is of a fairly self-sufficient community which provided for most of its own needs. There were workshops with tools and equipment to cope with most eventualities. Like most other manor houses of the period, Samlesbury Hall had its own brewhouse and bakehouse, with all the relevant equipment. There was a dairy with 'one frame: 5 milke troughes: 6 basons: 2 cheesefatts [?], one saltinge tubbe, 2 mugges, one churne: 2 collocks[e]: 2 piggins[f] & one stoole'... 'one cheese presse & 2 litle trests'. There was, of course, a wide range of kitchen utensils, many of which would not be out of place in a modern kitchen - '2 fryingepannes', 'spitts', 'fier irons', '4 [pot] hooks', '2 wooden platters, one pewter custard pott', '2 choppingeknives, one great knife, one pestell & a grater'.

The manor house at Samlesbury might have been a self-sufficient community, but it was certainly not isolated. It may be remembered that the traditional theory about the origins of Samlesbury Hall contends that this site was chosen because it was isolated and secluded enough to provide some security against Scottish raids. However, it now appears that the lord of the manor did not 'move house' after Bruce's raid; instead, the manor was split, and there was probably a separate manor house on each moiety. The Higher Hall had probably been the home of the Deuyas family for at least 50 years before Bruce's raid, and the other manor

A section of the original timber framing of the Great Hall, which has been left exposed and which can still be seen at the northern end of the Great Hall, as one approaches the main entrance of Samlesbury Hall. This section shows just how large the timber frames are.

Detail of part of the minstrels' gallery in the Great Hall. A quick comparison with the 1833 drawing of the old passage screen (see page 18) will show where parts of this gallery came from. In addition, as the V.C.H. says, 'a quantity of later Jacobean woodwork from old bedsteads and other furniture' was introduced, producing 'a rather strange and incongruous effect'.

---

[e]*collock*: a northern dialect word for a tub or similar vessel; a large pail, often with an erect handle and used for holding milk.

[f]*piggin*: a small pail, generally wooden; a milking pail, tub &c.

house or farmstead by the river (owned by the Hollands) was also occupied at this time - until Bruce's men raided it during their bloodthirsty shopping trip of 1322. It seems clear that Bruce's raid was not the reason for building Samlesbury Higher Hall.

Instead, the Deuyas, like the Southworths after them, probably lived at the Higher Hall because it was central to their estates, set in the midst of a prosperous, cultivated landscape. Samlebury Higher Hall might have been built in a clearing, surrounded by primeval swamps and forest, miles from anywhere, but it is unlikely. Most of the evidence, such as it is, points to fairly widespread and intensive cultivation of the land in late medieval Samlesbury. Certainly by the sixteenth century, and probably earlier, there was more land under the plough in Samlesbury than there is today. Rodgers found that in the early Tudor period some 56% of the productive land in the township was arable, as opposed to forest, meadow, pasture and so on. In 1595 there was said to be 1,000 acres under the plough in Samlesbury.[10] The Higher Hall lay at the heart of the township, not far from the busy Whalley road and well located to profit from the markets and fairs at Preston. Although the modern Preston to Blackburn turnpike did not bring a main road right to the front door of Samlesbury Hall (and right across one corner of the moat) until the 1820s, the Deuyas and Southworths almost certainly did not feel hopelessly cut off and isolated from civilisation.

If they did get bored, however, they could always relax with a little hunting. Our 1623 inventory lists 4 muskets and related equipment, and we know that there was a park - in all probability, a deer park - in Samlesbury in the sixteenth century, and perhaps earlier. Saxton's map of Lancashire shows it extending to the east of the hall in 1577, and

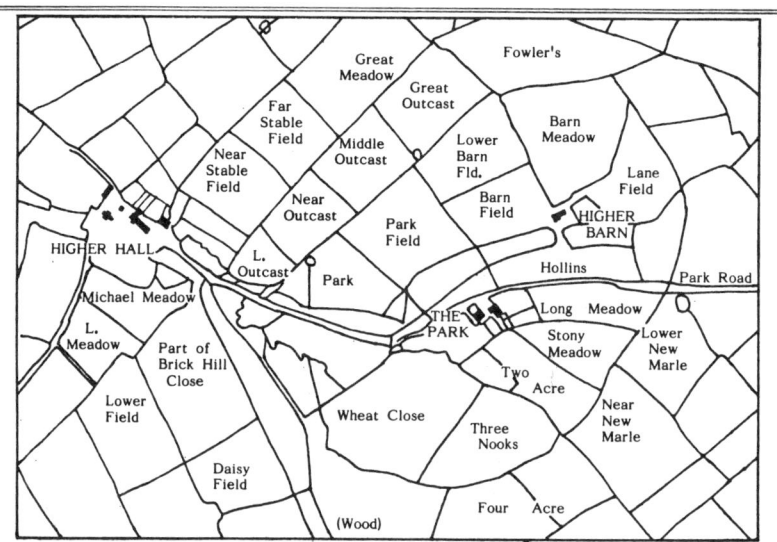

18th-century fields around Samlesbury Hall, from L.R.O. DDHj; the semicircular line of field boundaries around Park Farm and Lane can be seen clearly. This might just be the boundary of the earlier deer park.

several sixteenth-century documents, including the court leet records, mention the park, its park gates and its keeper.[11] The keeper of the park in 1592, as we have seen, was one John Singleton who lived in Samlesbury Hall itself.

The actual location of the park is uncertain, although there is strong evidence that it was just east of the Hall, extending on both sides of the modern Preston to Blackburn road, almost as far as Intack. Here, a lane from the Hall joins the main road. It passes Park Farm and is still called Park Road. The park gates mentioned in the court records might have stood at the points where this lane entered and left the park. Several eighteenth- and nineteenth-century maps show a uniform, almost semi-circular line of field boundaries sweeping south east from the Hall, then north east again to the new road, and enclosing a substantial area of undulating ground around Park Farm and Higher Barn (now converted to a fast-food restaurant selling roast chicken - perhaps they should start a new line in venison burgers!).[12] Within this area are two fields named on nineteenth-century maps as Park and Park Field; all the fields in this area could have been enclosed after the park was disused. Although new houses, Samlesbury airfield and the new (1824) road have all intruded on the site, part of the perimeter hedge is still there. The hedge looks undaunting today, but in places its accompanying ditch is quite deep. Four hundred years ago, it may well have been a sufficient barrier to freedom-loving deer enclosed within the park. There was a lodge within the park. We know that John Wright and his family were looking after Samlesbury Hall in 1592, and that they lived in the lodge. Presumably it was not too far from the Hall itself. Attempts have been made to show that the lodge, and by inference the park, was around New Hall on Cuerdale Lane, but the evidence for this is not very convincing.[13]

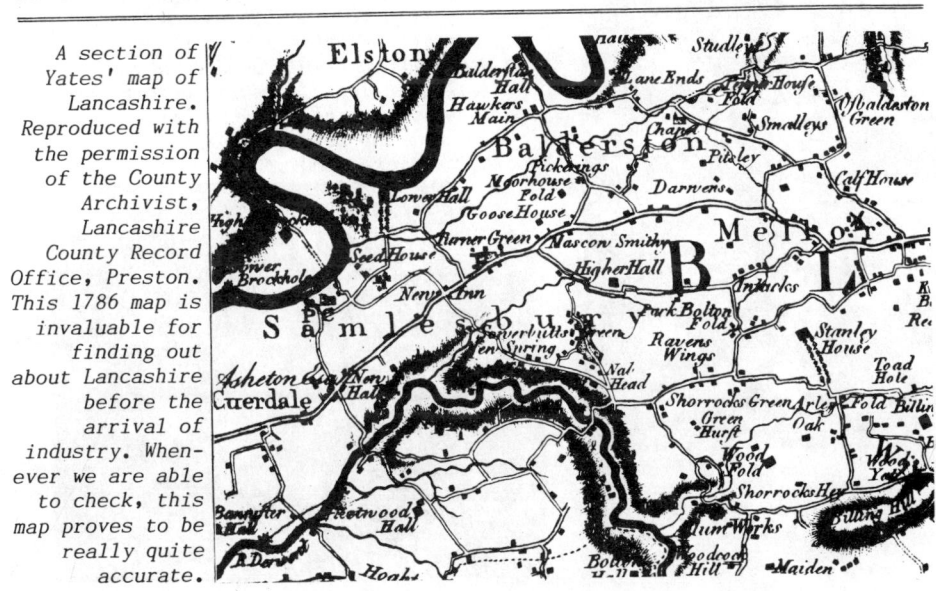

A section of Yates' map of Lancashire. Reproduced with the permission of the County Archivist, Lancashire County Record Office, Preston. This 1786 map is invaluable for finding out about Lancashire before the arrival of industry. Whenever we are able to check, this map proves to be really quite accurate.

Samlesbury Hall from the old courtyard. All of the lawn in the foreground and all of the buildings (except the small extension of the Great Hall to the right, which is modern) were included within the moat, which has now been filled in. It is probable that there were also buildings on the other sides nearest us, which have now disappeared.

Left: A detail of part of the south range wall facing the old courtyard. This section of the wall (at the left of the picture above) holds a clue about the missing parts of the Hall. The strip of narrow white motifs marks a clear break in the wall. To the left the wall has six quatrefoils, to the right, eight. The narrow strip has two large timber uprights on either side, which are far stronger than would seem to be required in that position. It is just possible that this line marks the position where another wall used to abut this one at right angles. It could indicate where an eastern wing joined this existing wall.
Below: One of the several sculpted panels on the old courtyard side of the Hall.

Above: Lintel of first-floor window, on the south range, nearest the bay window. The sculptures are supposed to depict, from left to right, a monk, Sir Thomas Southworth who rebuilt this part of the Hall in the middle of the sixteenth century, and a Roman emperor.
Left: Another sculpted panel from the south range of the Hall. All of these panels have been restored at least once and it is difficult to tell exactly when they were first made. On this picture, note the difference between the old wall timbers at the top, and some more recent wood at the bottom.

Right: The bay window, with the so-called 'priests' room' above. The bay window seems to have been added in the sixteenth century, as in several other Lancashire halls. Its use is slightly obscure, but it is thought that, apart from providing more light for the Great Hall, it could be used to display the family plate, or as a lady's bower. The stained glass in its windows was added in 1936, and it depicts the heraldic devices of 10 kings and queens of England. The roof of the small priests' room above extends back to join with the roof the Great Hall. On the inside, however, the enclosed angle which this creates is not obvious. One cannot see where the space is. This is usually thought to be the hiding hole discovered by royal officials in 1592. Today, one can see this hiding hole near the entrance to the priests' room.

SIR JOHN SOUTHWORTH

Historians know more about villains and wrong-doers than about anyone else in the past. Contrary to one school of thought, this is not because of any natural affinity or connection between historians and villainy, but rather because it is so much easier to find out about the things people did wrong than about almost any other aspect of their lives. People's misdeeds were far more likely to be recorded - in court and legal documents of all kinds - than were any of their other, more mundane activities. And, because more legal documents have survived than any other kind of record, we can find out more about things like crime, delinquency and sheer wickedness than about most other aspects of the ordinary lives of our ancestors.

Largely for this reason, Sir John Southworth of Samlesbury is famous.[a] Not that he was a particularly bad or evil man; nor did he commit any dastardly crimes. He found his way into the records because of his religion. Queen Elizabeth's privy council, the lord lieutenant and the Lancashire justices of the peace all kept a close eye on Sir John and his family. They wrote letters, lengthy reports and memoranda about him. What the authorities were so worried about was Sir John's refusal to accept the Reformation settlement of 1559. At a time when government demanded the religious conformity of all its subjects, it was extremely wary of anyone who openly opposed the established Church. The authorities regarded such opposition as dangerous both to the government and the country. Sir John Southworth, like many of his Lancashire neighbours, saw it all rather differently. He looked upon the new Protestant religion as no more than an unwelcome innovation, and he resolved to maintain his allegiance to the old Catholic religion of his forefathers. The official religion might have been changed, but Sir John Southworth saw no reason to change his own.

John Southworth's career in public service and as a soldier started well enough. His ambitions and lifestyle were fairly typical of most prominent country gentlemen of his time. Supervision of the family estates was combined with a varied social life and occasional service in official posts. John was twenty years old when his father, Sir Thomas Southworth, died in 1546, just a year after the renovation of parts of Samlesbury Hall had been completed. Shortly after he inherited the family estates, John Southworth married Mary Assheton, daughter of the prominent Lancashire knight, Sir Ralph Assheton of Middleton. Next year, 1547, John Southworth was on military service against the old enemy in Scotland, and he received his knighthood while he was there. Sir John was again in the North some years later, commanding a hundred Lancashire men; his superior officers recommended that his commission be extended and enlarged - Sir John's desire was 'that he might continue in service here with his hundred men and to have alsoe putt to his leading another hundred men. Hee says hee is a yonge man, and desirous to know s[er]vice in warr'. Three years later, he was again ordered north, this time to Berwick with 300 men, to keep a watchful eye on the Scots once more.[1]

---

[a] *This Sir John Southworth is not to be confused with B1. John Southworth who was martyred in 1654. See below, p.35.*

Sir John's career took another step forward when he was appointed high sheriff of Lancashire in 1561, an annual post which his father had held before him.[2] During Sir John's year of office, however, the first hint of the approaching religious troubles came when he was rebuked and threatened with a large fine of £40 for failing to execute warrants sent from the York High Commisssion which involved the arrest of some Roman Catholics in Lancashire.[3]

Soon the government was urging the bishops to seek out and prosecute the Catholics who failed to show their conformity by attending their local parish churches. The Bishop of Chester, in whose diocese Lancashire then was, was William Downham, 'a weak man, dominated by his sharp-tongued wife, and reluctant to offend the conservative gentry among whom he made his friends'.[4] He delayed and prevaricated; he was complacent about the religious situation in the county. Despite increasingly obvious and, to the government, alarming evidence to the contrary, he declared in 1568 that he 'found the people very tractable and obedient' to the new religious laws. Sir John Southworth, by now a noted Lancashire Catholic, was even allowed to continue in office as an ecclesiastical commissioner, despite his opposition to the very laws he was meant to be enforcing. The privy council, even Elizabeth herself, told Bishop Downham to proceed with greater urgency against the Catholics of Lancashire.[5]

Eventually, the council itself dismissed Southworth from the ecclesiastical commission, and summoned him to London to be interviewed and

Funerary armour of the Southworth family, which hangs on the northern wall at the sanctuary end of Samlesbury church.

The south range of Samlesbury Hall from the main road. When it was built, this road cut across one corner of the moat which used to surround the Hall.

questioned by Matthew Parker, the Archbishop of Canterbury. It was alleged that Sir John had broken 'the ecclesiastical laws and orders of this realm', that he had entertained Catholic priests in his home, that he had 'spoken against the present state of religion established by her majesty and the states of her realm in parliament' and had 'otherwise misbehaved' in matters of religion. The archbishop interviewed Sir John on 14 July, 1568, and

> 'offered him the form of submission prescribed by your honours [ie. the council]; he refused to submit himself to any such subscription; his conscience cannot serve him in most points of that order. He offereth to promise not to receive or sustain any such disordered persons as heretofore he hath sustained and holpen [helped]. He further seemeth to desire that he may be suffered to live according to his conscience, and desireth much to have licence to go over sea.'[6]

One authority states that Sir John did relent and sign the submission offered to him, but on 25 July Secretary of State Cecil made it clear that

> 'Sir John Southworth... cannot nor will be p[er]suaded to such conformity and subscription as wer meete. And therefore it is resolved that he shall remayne where he is [in custody], till tyme or good advisement and p[er]suasion may wyn and moove him to order.'[7]

However, the council was unwilling to invoke the full force of the law. The lords of the council thought 'it better... for things touching his conscience he be rather procured to be won by persuasion and good information than by process [of law] or other open manner of dealing'.[8] The government would have preferred it if Sir John could be converted

The interior of the Great Hall in about 1850, as sketched by Rimmer. The minstrels' gallery had been created by this date, using parts of the old passage screen (see page 18). This drawing also shows the roof in some detail. Picture courtesy of Mr L Brown.

willingly to Protestantism. Accordingly, Sir John was lodged with Edmund Grindal, then Bishop of London, in the hope that the good bishop's company and conversation might bring him to relent. Grindal reported, however,

> 'that I can do no good with Sir John Southworth for altering his opinion in religion. Besides my travail with him, Mr. Dean of [St.] Paul's, requested by me, hath conferred with him very oft, and hath used much courtesy and humanity towards him, and not without charge; which in reason might be a mean to move the said Sir John somewhat to relent. But the man is altogether unlearned, carried with a blind zeal without knowledge. His principal grounds are: "he will follow the faith of his fathers... [and] he will die in the faith wherein he was baptized &c".' [9]

The government gave up for a time. Sir John Southworth was released and allowed to return to Samlesbury where he could begin again to lead a normal life. But the authorities continued to keep an eye on his activities. His name often appears at or near the top of the lists of 'recusants' - those who failed to attend their local Protestant parish church. In 1574 the whole Southworth family was summoned to the ecclesiastical commission in York, but like many others they failed to attend and their case seems to have been dropped. Sir John was again reported to the council in 1576. [10]

Things got worse in the early 1580s. Government fears about a possible invasion by Catholic Spain were compounded by fear that the English Catholics were somehow in league with the queen's foreign enemies. In 1581 a new Act was passed by parliament which made it treason simply to acknowledge the Pope's authority in England. In theory at least, Catholicism became a capital offence. [11] Four Catholic priests were executed in the same year, and Sir John Southworth was one of the first of the Lancashire Catholics to be caught in the net of suspicion.

Stained glass window on eastern gable wall of St. Leonard-the-Less, Samlesbury.

The 'priest's room' above the bay window, Samlesbury Hall. Various stories are connected with this room, and several people have sensed a strange atmosphere in the room.

The Earl of Derby, who was lord lieutenant of Lancashire and the government's most important agent in the county, was told to arrest and confine Sir John Southworth to prison. In June, 1581, Sir John wrote to the privy council from the New Fleet prison in Manchester, asking 'that he might be suffered to repair & abyde at his owne house upon bonds for his forthcominge; or els to have a servant for his necessary uses, to attend upon him in the prison'.[12] Trusting Sir John's word that he would not abscond, the council authorised his release; on 25 February following, however, the council ordered him to report within thirty days to the Earl of Derby, who was ordered to 'commit him to the prison of Manchester... if you shall finde him to continue in his obstinacie'. The keeper of the prison, one Robert Worsley, was ordered to 'permitt the said Sir John, for the preservation of his health to walke & take the benefitt of the open aire in the gardens... so as he be not suffered to have conference with any person'.[13]

As part of the harsh law of 1581, recusants were to be fined the immense sum of £20 per month for as long as they failed to attend their local Protestant church. Many Catholics, especially in Lancashire, managed to keep their heads down and avoid these fines, but Sir John Southworth was too well known. The Act also laid down that one third of the fine would go to the person who brought information against any of the recusants. Some informers made quite a career of testifying against Catholics in this way. One such was Hugh Cuffe of London, who pleaded in the Exchequer that 'John Southworth of the parish of Blackburn, Lancashire, knight', had lived 'continuously in that parish from 19 March 1580/1 [the day after the enacting of the statute] until the... 12th day of January, and had not resorted at any time during that period to his

Lath and plaster panel found in poor condition in New Hall on Cuerdale Lane. The central panel was in about 150 pieces, but was repaired by an art master from Blackburn. It was unveiled in its present position above the door of the domestic chapel in Samlesbury Hall in 1941.

The interior of St. Leonard-the-Less, Samlesbury, looking east. Parts of the building date from the 14th century, when the church was probably enlarged to accommodate an increasing population. Most of what we see here is from the 16th century, at which time the arches and aisles were built, and the roof of the nave was heightened. Parts of this work can still be seen in the stonework. Note the fine set of box pews, the two-deck pulpit and the communion rail.

parish church or to any other church, chapel or usual place of common prayer'.[14] Sir John pleaded not guilty at the Exchequer in April, 1582, apparently arguing that there was some factual error in Cuffe's information to the court. Because of the difficulty involved in getting a Blackburn jury all the way to London (it then being the usual practice to draw a trial jury from one's neighbours and peers), the proceedings were adjourned to the Lancaster assizes on August 27, where Sir John Southworth was found guilty. After a further journey, this time to Hereford where judgement was read, Sir John was ordered to pay his fines of £180. Cuffe, the informer, received £60 of this. Informing on Catholics was thus a profitable activity, and Cuffe went on to testify against another 23 Catholic gentlemen from 12 counties.

If Sir John could possibly bring himself to look on the bright side after all that had happened, he might at least agree that these protracted lawsuits had allowed him some amount of liberty from Manchester prison. In 1584, not long after his return to prison, Sir John was released again and ordered to go and live in London. It was thought that his presence in Lancashire, where he was 'greatly allied and friended' was too dangerous. At the same time, it was thought unfair that he should be punished twice - by fine and imprisonment - for the same offence. Later, in 1586, he was allowed to travel to Bath for the sake of his health. He was 60 years old. He was quickly recalled from Bath, however, when the council was told that he had associated with Catholics there, and had reputedly converted a few Protestants as well. Sir John was back in Lancashire shortly afterwards, and it is interesting to note that throughout the crisis of the Spanish Armada, Sir John Southworth was an occasional guest at the house of the Earl of Derby.[15]

The financial burden of the 1581 Act was crippling. There is some reason to believe that the Southworth estates were not in a healthy position anyway, and the fines of £240 a year would quickly have bankrupted the family if they had been collected in full. According to valuations of Sir John's estates in 1577 and 1580, the fines actually exceeded his total gross income from his lands.[16]

By October, 1587, when the matter again came to the attention of the privy council, Sir John's debts from the arrears of his recusancy fines amounted to £1,060, an impossibly large sum. A commission was awarded for the seizure of all the Southworth lands 'but as [Sir John] himself affyrmeth, all his landes and leases are allreadye seysed for her Majestie'. There was nothing left to seize.[17]

Sketch of Samlesbury Hall in about 1850, when it was an inn, the Bradyll Arms. Not long after, it was bought by Joseph Harrison who restored the Hall and extended this wing at the left.

It was this desperate financial situation which in the end drove Southworth to take the only step that could save his estates. Faced with insuperable and ever-increasing debts, with the forfeiture of his estates, and with the intermittent imprisonment that must have been beginning to tell on his health, Sir John Southworth attended a Protestant church. His 'conversion' was a financial expedient. Sir John, and apparently most of his family and household, remained Catholics; occasional attendance at the local Protestant church (no doubt at St. Leonard-the-Less in Samlesbury) was the price he was obliged to pay for a peaceful life.

It also saved his estates. By letters patent dated 1st December, 1587, he received the queen's pardon, the restoration of his property and the remission of £700 of his arrears. As one privy councillor pointed out, however, 'the statute also requyreth upon his submission a contynuance of his conformitye in comminge to Dyvyne Service; otherwise he is to take no benefyte by his submission'. The government would not

Samlesbury Hall, with the main road to the left. This shows just how close the road is to the building.

excuse Sir John until he had shown his change of heart by attending Protestant church over a period of time. It was not until 1st July, 1592, that the remainder of his arrears (£360) was remitted. He also obtained a second pardon 'by reason of his continued conformity', vouched for by the Archbishop of Canterbury.[18]

Within five months, however, the elderly Sir John Southworth was again the subject of governmental inquisition. Despite Sir John's pretended conformity, he and his family continued to be reported for attending Catholic services. In 1586, one Thomas Sherples [sic] informed that six members of the Southworth family and more than 30 servants heard regular masses in Samlesbury. Sherples alleged that 'at the Lodge in Samlesburie Parke there be masses daily and Seminaries diverse resort thither, [such] as James Cowpe, Harrison, Bell and such like'. The privy council continued to receive worrying reports about the strength of Catholicism in Lancashire, and also on the laxness of the local authorities there to prosecute, or even to identify, offenders.[19] The council therefore ordered a search of Samlesbury hall. Richard Brereton, a local justice of the peace, was ordered

Fireplace in the entrance hall of Samlesbury Hall. Just beyond the grate is a hole in which it is said priests could take refuge.

'to be... on Tuisdaye next in the morning (an hower at the least before daye), at the howse and lodge of Sir John Sotheworthe, accompanied with a convenient nomber of suche trustie persons as youe thinke fitteste to take with youe, and to be stronglie furnished in suche sorte as youe shall thinke sufficiente; where youe shall make verie diligente, exacte and carefull searche in all chambers, loftes, studies, sellers, vawtes [cellars and vaults] and all other roomes and secrett or suspicious places of the said howse or other howses adjoyninge to the same, for any Jesuitt, semynarie preiste [sic], unknowne or suspected person that maye be founde there... [and for any] wrytinges, pamphellettes, papers or other suspicious or superstitious thinges... and such armour and weapons as youe shall fynde in the said howse.'[20]

This somewhat heavy-handed dawn raid was carried out on 21 November, 1592. It did not result in the discovery of any priests or seminaries. John Wright, one of Sir John's servants, 'being asked when he sawe anie Jesuite or seminarye priest in his master's howse, saith that he sawe none there for the space of five yeares last paste, and for the space of xiiii daies last paste [he] saith that he sawe noe unknowne person or straunger in his master's howse'. John Wright could well have been protecting his master during these interrogations. Perhaps the family had had advance warning of the raid; perhaps they managed to hide most of the evidence. We cannot be sure.

Various 'suspicious' items of clothing were found, however, including 'a gown without a pocket' which was nevertheless thought capable of concealing letters. More importantly, several books were found, including 'a treatise of schisme, shewing that all Cathlikes must absent themselves from hereticall conventicles, to witt theire protestant prayer and sermons', and a Rheims testament. In all, 13 'books of Papistrie' were discovered in various rooms of the house, indicating the close contact Sir John was able to maintain with recent Catholic writings from the continent. The search of Samlesbury Hall also brought to light 'a secrett vawlte over the dyninge chamber', usually associated with the 'hiding hole' in the roof of the Great Hall, by the minstrels' gallery. In this vault were found 'one canabie [a canopy?] to hange over the alter', 'two candlestickes of brasse of the fashion used in the time of superstition [ie. before the Reformation]', and 'fourteen images of divers fashions'.

Intack Cottage, to the east of the township. Recently restored, this delightful little cottage has several interesting features. The wide ground-floor windows may have lit the workshop of a handloom weaver.

Thus, Sir John Southworth was molested for his religious beliefs almost to the end of his life. He died, aged 69, on 3 November, 1595. Throughout everything, Sir John had pleaded his loyalty to the queen and the government, constantly refuting the taint of treason which the law placed on his religious beliefs. Both Sir John and his son-in-law, Bartholomew Hesketh, swore their obedience and loyalty in the year of the Armada; Sir John even asked to be entrusted with some public employment. The government did in fact recognise hie 'former good services' for the state, and the privy council thought that because of his former public employment, 'it could be contented that he recyved as much Favor as lawfully mighte be' while he was in prison.[21] This typifies the government's attitude. The laws under which Sir John Southworth was prosecuted were harsh, but their enforcement was lenient and sporadic, and Sir John was able to escape most of their most drastic consequences. The government preferred to persuade, rather than to bully, prominent Catholic gentlemen like Southworth. At his first demonstration of conformity to Protestantism in 1587 his enormous arrears of recusancy fines were remitted, and he was able to hand over his estates more or less intact to his son.

THE LATER SOUTHWORTHS

Sir John Southworth and his wife had ten children in all. Two of the four daughters married into other prominent Lancashire Catholic families. One of them, Margaret, married Bartholomew Hesketh of Aughton esquire, a zealous supporter of Edmund Campion, the famous Jesuit and one-time visitor to Samlesbury Hall. Three of Sir John Southworth's sons died young. The eldest surviving son, Thomas, was 36 years old when he succeeded his father in 1595. It had been rumoured that old Sir John had wanted to disinherit this son because he had been converted to Protestantism, and the privy council took the rumour seriously.[1] However, Thomas Southworth did inherit the Samlesbury lands, and he allowed his own son John and his wife Jane to occupy the Lower Hall, which had perhaps just been built. The present ruined building there could date from about this time, although it does look to be slightly later. It was the eldest son of this John Southworth, another Thomas, who eventually succeeded to the family estates in November, 1616. Presumably he would have moved to Samlesbury Higher Hall on inheriting the estates. Certainly, we know that the Lower Hall was sold off to the Walmsleys of Dunkenhalgh (who had already acquired that moiety of the manor some years earlier).

Lower Hall Farm, with the old Hall by the river to the right. The encroachments of the Ribble have eroded the bank here, damaging the old Lower Hall.

Old Sir John Southworth had two other sons. One, Gilbert, became a lawyer. The other, Christopher, followed in the religion of his father, studying to become a Catholic priest. For a time he was at the English College at Rome. He was arrested within four months of his return to England, however, and he spent periods of imprisonment in the Gatehouse and Wisbech castle.[2]

A closer view of all that remains of the Lower Hall today...

It was this Christopher Southworth who was said to be dubiously involved in the trial of the 'witches of Samlesbury' at Lancaster assizes in 1612. This trial came at the very height of the craze of prosecutions for alleged witchcraft in Lancashire, so famous in the Pendle area.[3] The case involved three women from Samlesbury, Jennet Brierley, Ellen Brierley and Jane Southworth

...and its only current residents!

33

The Lower Hall at the end of the 19th century. It appears to be of late 17th-century date, although its site could well be considerably more ancient than that.

(noted above, the widow of John Southworth of Lower Hall). The women were indicted:

> 'for that they and every of them felloniously had practised, exercised, and used diverse devillish and wicked Arts, called Witchcrafts, Inchauntments, Charmes, and Sorceries, in and upon one Grace Sowerbuts; so that by meanes thereof her bodie wasted and consumed, *contra formam statuti* &c...'

Grace, a 14-year-old girl who was closely related to the Brierleys, testified that one day she had seen her grandmother Jennet

> 'first in her owne shape, and afterwards in the likenesse of a black Dogge, with two legges, which Dogge went close to the left side of this Examinate [ie. Grace], till they came to a Pitte of Water, and then the Dogge spake, and persuaded this Examinate to drowne her selfe there, saying, it was a faire and easie death'

Grace also accused her aunt, Ellen Brierley, of causing the death of a child which had wasted away. The court then heard John Singleton, a servant of old Sir John Southworth - probably the keeper of the park noted above - testify that 'he had often heard his Old Master, Sir John Southworth now deceased, say, touching the late wife of John Southworth... That the said wife was as he thought an evill woman, and a Witch: and that he was sorry for her husband... for he thought she would kill him'.

Gradually, however, the truth appeared. Family and religious differences had been the root cause of the allegations. Eventually the prosecution's star witness, Grace Sowerbutts, retracted, saying 'she never did know, nor had seen any Devils as formerly she had alleaged'. She then admitted that Christopher Southworth, the Catholic priest 'to whom she had been sent to learne her prayers, did perswade, counsell and advise her' to bring the charges. Quite why Christopher Southworth should have wanted to bring false accusations of witchcraft against members of his own family is not known. However, when the court heard that all the accused women had been converted to Protestantism not long before the charges were brought, it was decided that Christopher Southworth had manufactured the allegations for religious reasons. There may have been more to it than that, but it seems clear that Christopher Southworth had used to prevalent witchcraft hysteria as a convenient way of pursuing his own religious and family disagreements.

Venturing to dwell a moment longer in the realm of the supernatural, we should pause to consider the famous ghost of Samlesbury Hall - the White Lady. Many sightings over the years - including some by normally 'sober' witnesses like military officers, bus drivers and greengrocers - have continued to add, if not to the venerable lady's plausibility, then certainly to her mystique and popularity. The story is a familiar one - of how a Catholic lady from a Catholic family fell in love with a Protestant gentleman, how the couple decided to brave the inevitable consequences and to elope together, and how their plot was foiled by the lady's brother who jumped out and killed the lover, whereupon the grief-stricken lady is supposed either to have retreated to a French nunnery or to have committed suicide. Her ghost has often been seen, pale and sorrowful, in the grounds of Samlesbury Hall - the best season, according to one source, being August, the supposed anniversary of the tragedy. Historically, we are not sure who this lady might have been, but in light of the religious tensions that existed in Samlesbury, it is not by any means an improbable story. As to the ghost, the present writer must account himself agnostic on such matters. However, many people have confirmed the story and many others have claimed to sense other spirits in the Hall, especially in the small room above the bay window.

On a similar theme, one might be forgiven for digressing in order to mention the goblins of Samlesbury church who, when the chapel was first being built, decided that the site chosen by the builders was unsuitable. Every night the goblins moved 'their carefully squared stones... to another and less elevated place', and every day the builders returned them to their original location... 'The wearied builders at length let the spirits have their own way, and when they commenced building on the site supernaturally chosen they were no longer interfered with'. [4]

It was perhaps not surprising that a Southworth would eventually come to grief for his religion. John Southworth - now St. John Southworth - was perhaps a nephew of old Sir John, though his early life and career are obscure. He studied at the Catholic college at Douai on the continent, and became a priest there in 1617. After several years of work in London, he was arrested and condemned to death in 1627. He was reprieved for a time and he served heroically for the people of London during the plague of 1636. After several more arrests for preaching his faith, his sentence was finally carried out at Tyburn on 28 June, 1654. He was executed for refusing to disavow his priesthood. [5]

The moat steps at the beginning of this century. [Picture courtesy of Mr L Brown].

Meanwhile back at Samlesbury the family fortunes were waning. Several heads of the family died young. Another John Southworth was lord in 1642 when the civil wars broke out. He was 35 years old, but he does not appear to have taken any part in the fighting. Like most Catholic gentlemen in Lancashire, he probably tried to maintain a neutral stance. Nevertheless, the parliamentarian sequestrators seized his estates, and long delayed their return despite continuous appeals from their owner. Robert Cunliff, one of the sequestrators, stated in November, 1651, that John Southworth 'had always been reputed a Papist till then recently he had [as they had heard] become conformable, but his wife then remained a Papist'.[6] For this, he was obliged to pay a composition fine of £358 18s 0d for the return of his estates - a great financial burden on an already encumbered inheritance.

Financial difficulties dogged the family. John Southworth had to mortgage Samlesbury Hall in 1666 to help pay the family debts. Shortly after he died in 1676, his son Edward had to sell the whole Southworth inheritance in Samlesbury to Thomas Bradyll of Portfield for £3,150. Part of the purchase money was paid direct to Southworth's creditors. Thus ended the long association of the Southworth family with Samlesbury. As we shall see, their departure heralded in a long period of uncertainty for the future of Samlesbury Hall.[7]

SAMLESBURY CHURCH AND TOWNSHIP

The intrepid reader who has persevered thus far will undoubtedly have been struck by the frequency of the references in preceding pages to Catholics and Catholicism. In fact, there were Protestants in Samlesbury, and the chapel of St. Leonard-the-Less did have a congregation. To be sure, many of those who attended the chapel in the early years might have done so just to avoid the recusancy fines which had so nearly crippled the Southworth family. Even so, it seems likely that Protestants were probably in the majority most of the time.

It is perhaps ironic that St. Leonard-the-Less was rebuilt just at the time when the final establishment of Protestantism in the country was to deprive the chapel of many of its congregation. In 1558 the Earl of Derby, presumably in his capacity as joint lord of the manor, wrote

> 'to al his loving friends... As I am credibly enformed, the church at Samesbury is in ruine & indangering people that resort to heare God's worde, I have thought good to move my loving friends to help with there charity towards the re-edifying thereof.'[1]

As we have seen, the first chapel at Samlesbury that we know about dates from the middle of the twelfth century.[2] Parts of the present building are clearly older than the rest, and are said to belong to a fourteenth-century rebuilding. The outline of this work can be seen at the gable ends. The church at that time was evidently the same length as today, though narrower. The main structure as seen today dates from the sixteenth century. At that time the roof was heightened and two aisles were added to the north and south of the nave. Some repairs have been undertaken since, and the tower was added at the end of the last century, but the building is mainly of the sixteenth century.

A very early photograph of Samlesbury chapel, taken before the Tower was built at the end of the last century. Also missing are the two porches over the doors on this side. The building as seen here must be very little changed from when it was built in the 16th century. A memorial arch now stands in the place of the gates.

It remains a delightful little church, with many interesting features, especially on the inside. These include a fine two-deck (originally three-deck) pulpit, a communion rail from the seventeenth century and a 'wonderfully complete' (the eulogy is Pevsner's) set of box pews which the parishioners thankfully managed to save when the church was again renovated at the end of the last century. They add a great deal of character to the interior. In 1790 the Bishop of Chester granted a licence to John Watson, owner of the Roacher cotton mill, to erect a gallery '18½ feet by 11 feet, with forms and a staircase to lead between the two pillars at the west end of the chapel of Samlesbury'.[3] The gallery was removed in 1884 to make way for an organ to be built against the window.

In 1650 parliamentary commissioners found that the local Protestants wanted Samlesbury to be made an independent parish, 'they being above one hundred Families and six myles distant from their p[ar]ishe church...'[4] It must have been disheartening for the curate at Samlesbury to know that so many of his parishioners sympathised with Catholicism. By the end of the seventeenth century, the Lower Hall had become a major focus for Samlesbury Catholics, taking over from the Higher Hall after the Southworths had sold up. In 1709 the Rev. John Holme of Blackburn wrote to the Archbishop of Canterbury regarding a Catholic bishop's visit to the Lower Hall:

> 'the number of Papists that were there was very great. Mr Hull, my curate at Samlesbury chapell, tells me that he sees multitudes goe that way past his house, some on foot, some on horseback, most of them with little children in their arms. But the greatest concourse of people was on Sunday, because the Bishop was to preach that day. The neighbouring Protestants seemed to take little notice of the matter, it being no novelty with them, the same Bishop having been there upon the same occasion about five years ago.'[5]

In 1767 'as correct and complete a List of the Papists... as can be obtained' was drawn up in Samlesbury by the minister, William Stockdale and the churchwardens, John Charnley and William Longfellows.

The Southworth arms on one of the three old chimnies of Samlesbury Hall. A section of the early brickwork can also be seen.

They named 351 men, women and children in their list.[6] As table 2 shows, the nineteenth-century census returns reveal wide fluctuations in population at that time, so it is difficult to estimate what percentage of the population those 351 Catholics represented in 1767. Clearly, though, it is a fairly high proportion.

Perhaps of more interest is the fact that the 1767 list gives the chief trade or employment of each person. This is very useful indeed for indicating the nature of Samlesbury's economy at this time. By far the most noticeable feature is the very high proportion of people engaged in textile manufacturing, both weaving and spinning. Unless the Catholics named in this list were far more likely to take up these occupations than the rest of the population - which is highly improbable - then this list suggests that domestic industry was already crucial to the local economy in 1767. The following extract illustrates how the list is compiled:

'Jeremiah Smith weaver aged 42, wife 40 & a Boy
Bernard Smith weaver, aged 50, Wife 52, 3 Daughters C[otton]
    Spinners
Stephen Vaw Carpenter, aged 70
Wm Wesley Weaver, aged 28, Wife 28, & 1 Boy
Henry Brown Weaver, aged 35, wife 36 & 2 Boys & 3 Girls
George Sharplyes Weaver, aged 60, wife 58, & One Daughter a
    Cotten Spinner aged 23.'

If it is safe to regard each entry on each new line as a separate household, then only 21 out of 108 (a mere 19·4%) of Catholic households did not have any member working either as a spinner or weaver. No fewer than 54 male heads of households (68%) were handloom weavers, and many other entries begin with women on their own described as cotton

TABLE 2

POPULATION OF SAMLESBURY
1801 - 1951

This graph indicates the wide fluctuations in population in Samlesbury, 1801 to 1951. It shows a sharp rise early in the nineteenth century, associated with the growth of domestic industry, especially of handloom weaving. From a peak in 1821, the population fell, probably because many people went to nearby towns like Preston in search of better-paid work in the cotton mills and other factories. Only between the wars did the population begin to rise again. More recently, the numbers have been fairly steady, just over 1,000 people.

spinners; perhaps these were households where the husband was a Protestant and therefore not included in our list. In most cases the father wove while the daughters and occasionally the wife spun. It is also significant that the only yarn mentioned by name is cotton. It has usually been thought that cotton did not take over from linen as the principal cloth until later in the century.[7]

The early census returns confirm the general situation. The first set of returns, for 1801, divides the population of 1,664 into 1,606 persons 'chiefly employed in Trade, manufactures and handicraft' and only 56 persons employed mainly in agriculture. In 1821, when the census shows the highest ever population in Samlesbury, 20 families (a better guide than the 1801 figures which included children in the calculations) worked in agriculture, compared with 302 in trade and manufacture. There were a large number of handloom weavers even in 1851.[8]

Many of the people listed in both the 1767 Catholic list and the early census returns probably came to domestic industry as a sideline, at least at first. Most will originally have been agricultural workers. It is interesting that the 1767 list contained only two or three people who had not been born in Samlesbury. The large number of weavers and spinners is not accounted for by immigration from elsewhere. Many people may also have combined textile work with other activities; the lists refer only to their chief employment, and we know from other areas that many probably also worked part-time on the land, often on their own plots. This is perhaps supported in Samlesbury by the lack of the distinctive, purpose-built weavers' cottages so common elsewhere in central Lancashire.[9] Most old farmhouses and cottages, however, do show tell-tale signs of handloom weaving. Many of them have the typical long, low windows used to light the ground floor loom-shops. Such buildings seem

The 14th-century bell which has now been hung above the eastern door to Samlesbury church.

to have been converted to the new use, rather than being specially built for weaving, suggesting at least an initial period when the occupants worked both in agriculture and in textiles.

Table 2 shows the scale and extent of the population decline in Samlesbury towards the middle of the nineteenth century. Mainly this was because more and more young people went to the towns - Preston, Blackburn and others - to find work. Few new factories opened in Samlesbury itself to compensate for the decline of the old domestic handloom weaving industry. Two small textile factories were built, at Roach

Bridge and Samlesbury Bottoms, on the fairly large and fast-flowing river Darwen to the south of the township. Even at their height, however, these mills did not employ a large number of hands. Later, they both changed from cotton spinning to the more profitable trade of paper making.

As the number of people living in Samlesbury gradually declined, a higher proportion of those who remained worked on the land. By this time other areas had taken over as the principal agricultural regions of Lancashire, and Samlesbury has never regained the importance it once had in this field. However, trade directories for the latter half of the last century show that the Samlesbury economy was again predominantly rural, and so it has remained. Despite being close to both Blackburn and Preston, Samlesbury has managed to avoid being swallowed up by its larger neighbours. Apart from some ribbon development along the main road, there has been little new building. Several large industrial concerns have now taken up residence in the township, including some large sewage works, a modern brewery and an aerodrome which in headier days was once intended to become an international airport.[10] It now has an important aircraft works instead. With these, the new road and the motorway, the face of Samlesbury has changed again, although its essentially rural character remains.

Samlesbury Bottoms, the site of an early cotton spinning mill. Near here also stood the old water-powered manorial corn mill. Further downstream, the river Darwen also powered another cotton mill at Roach Bridge.

SAMLESBURY HALL: 'THE VICISSITUDES OF FORTUNE'

Any domestic building which is four or five hundred years old is bound to have seen many changes and many ups and downs. We have seen how the ownership of Samlesbury Hall changed several times. From 1679 there have only been a few years during which the Hall has had a resident owner. Inevitably the building underwent many adaptations and changes of use as each tenant modified it to suit his own needs. However, as Mr C. R. Peers, Chief Inspector of Ancient Buildings for the Ministry of Works noted in 1925, 'As a result of my visit to Samlesbury I am more than ever impressed with the value and interest of the Hall. In spite of the vicissitudes of fortune which it has endured, there is quite an unusual amount of ancient detail in it, and, moreover, as far as can be seen, the old work is in a very satisfactory condition'.[1]

By the beginning of the last century, the fabric of Samlesbury Hall was decayed. In 1824 the new road was built right up against one corner of the south range of the Hall, evidently in order to maintain the straightness of the road's line.[2] 'Indeed the road cuts across the spacious moat which formerly surrounded this venerable seat of the Southworths, and almost touches one corner of the building...'[3] It was probably the increased traffic brought by the new road that led to the Hall's conversion into an inn, the Bradyll Arms. It was at this time that the Hall underwent its first bout of 'restoration'. This 1835 work apparently saved the building from near ruin, but at a high cost to much of its ancient detail.[4]

For a time, part of the Hall became a girls' boarding school. The original headmistress's grandson wrote to the local paper in 1926 explaining that his grandmother had taken this initiative 'in order to augment the income which was necessitated by her husband being there stricken with paralysis; and there having been seven children...'[5] In 1851 the 'Old Hall' is listed in the census returns as accommodating two resident families, the Crooks who farmed 70 acres, and the Earnshaws who combined farming and textile work.

Shortly afterwards, the Hall was bought by Joseph Harrison, who spent large sums of money on restoring the building. He extended the main south range at its western end, while 'in the internal decorative work [Harrison] had the services of Mr Shaw F.S.A., author of The Decorative Arts of the Middle Ages',[6] and many parts of the Hall today are the product of their work together. Before long, however, the future of Samlesbury Hall was again plunged into uncertainty. At one stage, in about 1911, it was even rumoured that the whole building might be dismantled and sent to America. The Hall had many admirers, however, and a vigorous campaign to buy and save it was begun by a number of local people. Eventually a Trust was established and the money was raised. Several suggestions were made for its subsequent use, including one as the headquarters of the new diocese of Blackburn. 'The most popular scheme', however, was 'the establishment of a Lancashire museum, where... copies of the original models of important patents in Lancashire's industrial progress... may be retained'.[7] Through the hard and dedicated work of many people, Samlesbury Hall has been further restored and repaired, and has become one of the most important tourist features of the Ribble Valley. At last, its future seems secure.

An ivy-covered Samlesbury Hall in the 1920s. [courtesy of Mr L Brown].

Abbreviations

B.M.	British Museum, London; Manuscripts Department
Croston	J. Croston, *A History of the Ancient Hall of Samlesbury* (London, 1871)
C.S.P.D.	*Calendar of State Papers, Domestic Series*
Eaton	R. Eaton, *A History of Samlesbury in the Hundred of Blackburn* (Blackburn, 1936)
L.R.O.	Lancashire Record Office, Bow Lane, Preston
M.C.L., Towneley MSS	Manchester Central Library, Archives Dept., LI/51/1/15
P.R.O.	Public Record Office, Chancery Lane, London
V.C.H.	*Victoria County History, Lancashire* (1912).

Notes

Pre-history

[1] *V.C.H.*, vi, 303-4

[2] T. Garlick, *Roman Lancashire* (Whitehaven,1977); G.D.B. Jones, 'The Romans in the North West', *Northern History*, iii, (1968); A.C. Hodge and J.F. Ridge, *Ribchester: A Short History and Guide* (Preston, 1984); E.E. Pickering, 'Roman Walton-le-Dale', *Trans. Hist. Soc L. & C.*, cix (1957), pp. 1-46.

[3] C. Hardwick, *History of Preston and its Environs* (Preston, 1857), 74-6; F. Banks, *The Problem of Cuerdale* (offprint from *The Numismatic Gazette*, Nov-Dec, 1966).

[4] J. Hallam, 'Central Lancashire New Town Archaeological Survey' (pre-publication edition, 1980).

[5] J.G. Evans, *The Environment of Early Man in the British Isles* (Elek, 1975); R. Muir, *Shell Guide to Reading the Landscape* (London, 1981).

[6] E. Ekwall, *English Place-Names* (4th ed., London, 1960); A.H. Smith, *English Place-Name Elements* (Cambridge, 1956), ii, 100. Eaton discusses the various possibilities, 3-5.

[7] H.C. Darby, *The Domesday Geography of Northern England* (Cambridge, 1962). E.B. Demerast, 'Inter Ripam et Mersham', *English Historical Review*, xxxviii (1923), pp. 161-70.

The Medieval Manor of Samlesbury

[1] *V.C.H.*, vi, 310. See below, pp. 36-7.

[2] Eaton, 6. For the connection with Alston, see L.R.O. DDHo Deed Book, no. 388; *Lancs. Inq. & Extents (Record Soc. L & C)*, i, 16, 54, 58, 75.

[3] The genealogical evidence is covered well by Croston, Eaton and the *V.C.H.*; there is no need to repeat their work here.

[4] M.C.L. Towneley MSS, 1736.

[5] This theory seems to have derived from Eaton's comments about the township's early manorial history, but Eaton himself maintains that this is no more than a possible sequence of events. Croston is even more non-committal. Most later writers have seized upon Eaton's theory, and it has now been almost accepted as historical fact.

[6] *V.C.H.*, iv, 92-3. Croston also gives many details about the Hollands, pp. 25 *seq*.

[7] M.C.L. Towneley MSS, passim. See also Eaton, 10, 16; R. Cunliffe Shaw, *The Royal Forest of Lancaster* (Preston, 1956), 242; R. Somerville, *History of the Duchy of Lancaster, vol i (1265-1603)*, (London, 1953, 21 n.5; P.R.O., DL 41/1/37; *Coucher Book of Whalley*, ed. W.A. Hulton, Chetham Soc., o.s., x, xi, xvi, xx (1847...), x, 121-2; *Lancs. Inq. & Extents*, i, 313, 314; ii, 12.

[8] The best survey of this period is G.H. Tupling, 'South Lancashire in the Reign of Edward II', *Chetham Soc.*, third series, i, (1949).

[9] *Lancs. Inq. & Extents*, ii, 144.

[10] 'while Robert de Leyburn was sheriff of Lancaster...there came a certain Roger de Astynthwayt, a clerk, with a certain commission of the lord king to take oats... etc...to the king's use', G.H. Tupling, *op. cit.*, 131. Ironically, Leybourn had been instructed to raise troops in Lancashire to oppose any Scottish incursion, *ibid.*, xxxv.

[11] Coram Rege Roll, No. 254, quoted in *ibid.*, 133. See also R. Cunliffe Shaw, *op. cit.*, 130-1.

[12] For several years after his victory over Edward II at Bannockburn in 1314, Bruce

had been raiding the north of England, partly in an attempt to put pressure on the English king to retract his claims to sovereignty over Scotland. The raids were not entirely gratuitous, therefore, and their primary motivation was political, G.W.S. Barrow, *Robert Bruce* (Edinburgh, 1976). The main source for Bruce's raid is the *Chronicon de Lanercost*, printed by the Maitland Club. The Penwortham inquest is printed in *Lancs. Inq. & Extents*, ii, 162-3.

[13] *Ibid.*, T. Whitaker, *A History of...Whalley* (2 vols., London, 1872-6), ii, 344.
[14] *Coucher Book of Whalley*, 121-2; Eaton, 11, 117.
[15] M.C.L., Towneley MSS, 1741, 1758; *Lancs. Inq. & Extents*, ii, 12.
[16] Croston, 147.
[17] *Lancs. Inq. & Extents*, ii, 144; *V.C.H.*, vi, 304 n.16; iv, 92-3.
[18] M.C.L., Towneley MSS, 1775.
[19] L.R.O., DDX 388/3, 4. This, the original Holland moiety, was sold to Judge Walmsley of Dunkenhalgh in 1601. Eaton, 56-8. L.R.O. DDPt 35; *V.C.H.*, vi, 306.
[20] E. Crompton, *The Soils of the Preston District of Lancashire* (Harpenden, 1966), 64-5.
[21] H.B. Rodgers, 'Land Use in Tudor Lancashire: The Evidence of the Final Concords, 1450-1558', *Institute of Brit. Geographers, Trans. & Papers*, xxi (1955), pp.79-97. R. C. Shaw concludes that 'whereever details of the agrarian system are available it is certain that by the 13th century all the numerous vills [townships] in the western arable belt of Lancashire and its prolongations eastward up the Ribble and Lune valleys were fully cultivated', *op. cit.*, 346.
[22] The literature on this subject is large. For a recent study of techniques for part of Cheshire, see R. Williams, 'Aerial Archaeology and the Evidence for Medieval Farming in West Cheshire', *Trans. Hist. Soc. L. & C.*, cxxiii (1984), pp. 1-24. See also J.Z. Titow, *English Rural Society, 1200-1350* (London, 1969), 33-6, 71-2.
[23] *Record Soc. L. & C.*, xxxi (1896).
[24] W.A. Abram, 'The Rolls of Burgesses at the Guild Merchant...of Preston', *Record Soc. L. &. C.*, ix (1884); G.H. Tupling, 'The Origins of Markets and Fairs in Medieval Lancashire', *L. & C. Antiq. Soc.*, xlix (1933); R. Lennard, 'Manorial Traffic and Agricultural Trade in Medieval England', *Jnl. Agric. Econ. Soc.*, v, (1938).
[25] The court leet had to threaten the ferryman with a fine for negligence in the 16th century, L.R.O. DDX 1119/6/10; DDX 336/4; DDH 436.
[26] *V.C.H.*, vi, 304-7; R. Cunliffe Shaw, *op. cit.*, 166, 190.

Sir Thomas Southworth and Samlesbury Hall

[1] The present writer is no expert on medieval vernacular architecture. I have relied heavily on the work of N. Pevsner, *The Buildings of England, North Lancashire* (1969), 18-19, 216-7. The *V.C.H.*, vi, 307-10 is also useful.
[2] R. Somerville, *History of the Duchy*, i, 291 n.1.
[3] The letter is quoted at length by Eaton.
[4] L.R.O. WCW, Thomas Southworth of Samlesbury, esquire, 1623. For a useful discussion of this type of document, see O. Ashmore, 'Household Inventories of the Lancashire Gentry, 1550-1700', *Trans. Hist. Soc. L. & C.*, cx (1958), pp.59-105.
[5] For a recent archaeological survey of this kind by a local group, see *Old Cottam Hall: An Archaeological Survey* (Preston, 1985).
[6] See below pp. 31-2.
[7] O. Ashmore, *art. cit.*, 59-61.
[8] J.J. Smith, 'Lancashire and Cheshire Houses: Some Problems of Architectural and Social History', *Archaeolog. Jnl.*, cxxvii (1970), pp.156-81.
[9] *V.C.H.*, vi, 309.
[10] H.B. Rodgers, 'Land Use in Tudor Lancashire', 95. Croston reprints a survey of the Southworth estates at the time of Sir John Southworth's death in 1595, pp. 71 *seq*.
[11] L.R.O. DDX 1119/6/6, 1119/6/7. See also the map in L.R.O. DP 243.
[12] L.R.O. DDX 336/23 (estate map c.1757). DDX 1119/9/2 appears to be the schedule for this map. See also the maps in L.R.O. DDHj (Acc. no. 4706), Samlesbury estate maps, early 19th century. I am most grateful to Barbara Sharp for this reference. See also the tithe map, L.R.O. DRB 1/172.
[13] Eaton says that the New Hall has been established as the Lodge almost beyond doubt, but cites no evidence to support this.

Sir John Southworth

[1] *The Lancashire Lieutenancy under the Tudors and Stuarts*, Chetham Soc., xlix & l (1859), 4, 9, 18-19, 46; Croston, 54; *V.C.H.*, vi, 306.
[2] P.R.O. DL 42/22 f.164v; 42/23 f.253.
[3] C. Haigh, *Reformation and Resistance in Tudor Lancashire* (Cambridge, 1975), 213; R. Somerville, *History of the Duchy*, i, 463-4.
[4] C. Haigh, *op. cit.*, 251 and *cap.* 16 passim.
[5] *Ibid.*, 223; *C.S.P.D.*, *1547-80*, 203, 305, 307. The Bishop of Chester did present Sir John for his defaults but apparently not until November, 1568, *ibid.*, 322; F.O. Blundell, *Old Catholic Lancashire, 1550-1850* (London, 1941), iii, 28. See also P. Caraman, *The Other Face: Catholic Life under Elizabeth I* (1960), pp. 194-6. It had been rumoured that Sir John had been party to secret Catholic conferences in York, Croston, 57
[6] *The Correspondence of Matthew Parker*, eds. J. Bruce and Rev. T. Thomason, (Parker Society, 1853), 330-1; *C.S.P.D.*, *1547-80*, Addenda, 47
[7] *Correspondence of Matthew Parker*, quoting Strype, *Parker*, Bk.iii, *cap.* 19. Cecil's letter is in B.M. Add. MSS, 32,091, f.251.
[8] *Correspondence of Matthew Parker*, 329-30
[9] *The Remains of Edmund Grindal*, ed. W. Nicholson, (Parker Society, 1843). 305.
[10] C. Haigh, *op. cit.*, 262; *V.C.H.*, vi, 306.
[11] For a useful recent discussion of the Act and its implications, see A. Dures, *English Catholicism: Continuity and Change* (London, 1893), 28-34.
[12] F. Peck, *Desiderata Curiosa* (2 vols. in 1, London, 1779), 105-6.
[13] *Ibid.*, 114-5; W.R. Trimble, *The Catholic Laity in Elizabethan England, 1558-1603* (Cambridge, Mass., 1964), 112. Sir John complained about his treatment and the conditions in prison, and the privy council intervened after receiving a report on the matter, *Desiderata Curiosa*, 138; Croston, 65-8; *C.S.P.D.*, *1581-90*, 50.
[14] A full account of these proceedings can be found in *Recusant Roll*, No. 2 *(1593-4)*, ed. H. Bowler, Catholic Record Society, vol. lvii (1965), xxvi-xx, xxxi. Bowler draws much of his evidence from the records of the Queen's Remembrancer.
[15] Trimble, *op. cit.*, 129; *Desiderata Curiosa*, 150. Apparently Sir John Southworth had been in Bath - a well-known Catholic meeting place - in 1569, at which time he was held 'in great admiration' by the 'hinderers of God's word and Gospel, Croston, 57-8. *Stanley Papers*, part 2, Chetham Soc. o.s., xxxi (1853), 31, 77, 124.
[16] In 1569, Sir John was said to 'stand Indebted to divers persons in divers greate Sommes of money', M.C.L., Towneley MSS, 1046, 1048. In 1577, he was valued at £200 *per annum* in lands, Trimble, *op. cit.*, 206.
[17] *Recusant Documents from the Ellesmere MSS*, ed. A.G. Petti, Catholic Record Society, lx (1968), 29.
[18] Bowler, *op. cit.*, xxxi; Petti, *op. cit.*, 29.
[19] B.M. Harl. MSS, 360, fos.32v-33. Sections of this document are quoted in W.A. Abram, *A History of Blackburn* (Blackburn, 1877). *C.S.P.D.*, *1581-90*, 165, 297; C. Haigh, *op. cit.*, part III, passim.
[20] The fullest extracts are printed in Petti, *op. cit.*, 37-41. Parts are also printed in the Camden Society, *Egerton Papers*, xii (1840), 163-6.
[21] Croston, 65-7.

The Later Southworths

[1] Peck, *Desiderata Curiosa*, 149.
[2] A.O. Meyer, *England and the Catholic Church under Queen Elizabeth* (2nd edition, London, 1967), 497, 514; P Caraman, *Henry Garnet, 1555-1606* (London, 1964), 273; C. Haigh, *op. cit.*, 279; Croston, 83; *C.S.P.D.*, *1581-90*, 392.
[3] T. Potts, *The Wonderful Discovery of Witches...*, ed. J. Crossley, Chetham Soc., o.s., vi (1845); Croston, 110-119.
[4] The story is given in the *Blackburn Times*, 13 August, 1904.
[5] There is a fairly wide, but scattered literature about this John Southworth. The main work is E.E. Reynolds, *John Southworth, Priest and Martyr* (London, 1962); J.J. Delaney and J.E. Tobin, *Dictionary of Catholic Biography* (New York, 1961) gives a few more details.
[6] *Royalist Composition Papers*, Record Soc. L. & C., Vol vi, part 1, 115-8.
[7] Croston, 140-1, 149; B.G. Blackwood, *The Lancashire Gentry and the Great Rebellion*,

Chetham Soc., cxxv (1978), 114, 149 n.20.

Samlesbury: Church and Township

[1] Croston, 42, from Kuerden's MS in Chetham's Library, Manchester, p. 497.
[2] For Samlesbury church, see *V.C.H.*, vi, 311-2; G. Clayton, *St. Leonard-the-Less, Samlesbury* (Samlesbury, n.d.); N. Pevsner, *op. cit.*, 216.
[3] L.R.O. DDH 587/595.
[4] For a copy of the report, see L.R.O. DDCm 2/15.
[5] Quoted by Blundell, *Old Catholic Lancashire*, iii, 33-4. See Eaton, 135-6, for other visits to Samlesbury by prominent Catholic churchmen.
[6] The lists are printed by the *Catholic Record Society*, eds. E.S. Worrall, 'Returns of Papists, 1767, Diocese of Chester', Occasional Papers, 1 (1980), pp. 95-6.
[7] The earliest reference I have found to cotton in Samlesbury is 1722, when William Sumner of Samlesbury is described as 'cotton weaver', L.R.O. DDH 587; care must be exercised, however, as in the early period the terms 'cotton' or 'Manchester cotton' could actually refer to wool, N. Lowe, *The Lancashire Textile Industry in the Sixteenth Century*, Chetham Soc., third series, xx (1972). See also A.P.Wadsworth and J. de La Mann, *The Cotton Trade and Industrial Lancashire, 1600-1780* (Manchester 1931).
[8] The importance of the domestic textile industry is confirmed by parochial records, Eaton, 178.
[9] J.G. Timmins, *Handloom Weavers' Cottages in Central Lancashire*, (Lancaster, 1977).
[10] The scheme to develop Samlesbury aerodrome into an international airport was aired in a 1946 planning document entitled *Towards a Prouder Preston*; like many of the other ideas contained in this document, it was quickly forgotton.

Samlesbury Hall: 'The Vicissitudes of Fortune'

[1] *Blackburn Times*, 19 December, 1925.
[2] For the new road, see L.R.O. DDHj (Acc. no. 4706); DDX 1119/13/7.
[3] From a letter of 1830, quoted in the *Blackburn Times*, 19 April, 1924.
[4] *V.C.H.*, vi, 307.
[5] *Blackburn Times*, 6 February, 1926.
[6] *Ibid.*, 13 August, 1904.
[7] *Ibid.*, 6 June, 1925. The early work and activities of the Samlesbury Hall Trustees are described by Eaton, 230-3. See also *Blackburn Times*, passim.

Index

Alston, 1
Assheton, family, 24
  Mary, 24
  Sir Ralph, 24
Balderston, 4
Bath, 29, 44 n.15
Bell, Mr., 31
Blackburn, i, 20, 21, 29 39, 40
Bradyll, Thomas, 36
Brereton, Richard, 31
Brierley,
  Ellen, 33-4
  Jennet, 33-4
Brockholes, Higher, 2, 11
Bruce, Robert, 6, 8-9, 19

Campion, Edmund, 33
Cecil, William, 26
census returns, 38-9
cotton industry, 38-40
Cowpe, James, 31
Crooks, family, 41
Cuerdale
  hoard, 1
  Lane, 21
Cuffe, Hugh, 28-9
Cunliff, Robert, 36

Dean, Mr., 27
deer park, 20-1
  lodge, 21, 31
Deuyas, family, 9, 12, 19
  Alice, 10, 11
  Cecily, 4
  John, 4
  Sir John, 11
  Nicholas, 8-9
  Nicholas, 11
Domesday book, 3
Downham, William (Bishop of Chester), 25
Dublin, 1

Earnshaw, family, 41
Edward II, 6
Elizabeth I, 24
Elston, 1, 4

Fishwick, 2

Grindal, Edmund (Bishop of London), 27

Harrison, Mr., 31
Harrison, Joseph, 41
Henry VIII, 12
Hereford, 29
Hesketh, Bartholomew, 32, 33
Hindley, 1
Hoghton, family, 10
Holden, William de, 8
de Holland, family, 6-9, 19-20
  Elizabeth, 4, 6
  Robert, 4
  Sir Robert, 4, 6-11

Lancaster
  assizes, 29, 33
Leybourn, Robert, 7-8
Leofwin, 1

Manchester, 28, 29

Osbaldeston, 4

Parker, Matthew (Archbishop of Canterbury), 26
passage screen, 18
Penwortham, 2, 8
Preston, 2 (bis), 9, 10, 20-21, 39, 40

Ribble
  ferry, 11
  river, 1, 3, 4,
  valley, 1, 2, 4, 10
Ribchester, 1, 4
ridge and furrow, 10
Rufford, 18

Salesbury, 4
Samlesbury, passim
  aerodrome, 21, 40
  church, 4, 11, 30, 36-7
  earliest hall, 4, 6, 12
  Higher Hall, 4, 6, 9, 12-20, 31-2, 40-1
  White Lady of, 35
  Lower Hall, 4, 9, 33-4, 37
  New Hall, 21
de Samlesbury family
  Avina, 4
  Gospatric, 1, 3, 4,
  Margaret, 4
  Roger, 4
  William, 4
Sherples, Thomas, 31
Singleton, John, 15, 34
Southworth, family
  Christopher, 33-4
  Edward, 36
  Gilbert de (snr.), 10, 11
  Gilbert de (ygr.), 11
  Gilbert (lawyer), 33
  Jane, 33-4
  John, 11
  John (Lower Hall), 33
  John, 36
  Sir John, 24-32, 34
  St. John, 35
  Margaret, 33
  Thomas (inventory of), 14-19, 33
  Sir Thomas, 12-23, 25
Sowerbutts, Grace, 34
Spain, 27
Spanish Armada, 30, 32
Stanley, Henry (4th Earl of Derby), 28
Stockdale, William, 37
Swain, 1

Thomas, Earl of Lancaster, 6

Upholland, 6

Walton-le-Dale, 1, 2, 10
  church, 7
Watson, John, 37
Whalley Abbey, 9, 12-13
Wigan, 1
Worsley, Robert, 28
Wright, John, 21, 31

York, 1